T0303983

ROUTLEDGE LIBRARY EDITIONS:
THE ECONOMICS AND BUSINESS OF
TECHNOLOGY

Volume 21

INDUSTRIAL PRODUCT INNOVATION

INDUSTRIAL PRODUCT INNOVATION

Organisation and Management

F.A. JOHNE

Routledge
Taylor & Francis Group

LONDON AND NEW YORK

First published in 1985 by Croom Helm Ltd

This edition first published in 2018
by Routledge
2 Park Square, Milton Park, Abingdon, Oxon OX14 4RN

and by Routledge
711 Third Avenue, New York, NY 10017

Routledge is an imprint of the Taylor & Francis Group, an informa business

British Library Cataloguing in Publication Data
A catalogue record for this book is available from the British Library

ISBN: 978-1-138-50336-6 (Set)
ISBN: 978-1-351-06690-7 (Set) (ebk)
ISBN: 978-0-8153-8395-6 (Volume 21) (hbk)
ISBN: 978-1-351-20443-9 (Volume 21) (ebk)

Publisher's Note
The publisher has gone to great lengths to ensure the quality of this reprint but
points out that some imperfections in the original copies may be apparent.

Disclaimer
The publisher has made every effort to trace copyright holders and would welcome
correspondence from those they have been unable to trace.

Industrial Product Innovation

ORGANISATION AND MANAGEMENT

DR F.A. JOHNE

CROOM HELM
London & Sydney
NICHOLS PUBLISHING COMPANY
New York

© 1985 F.A. Johne
Croom Helm Ltd, Provident House, Burrell Row,
Beckenham, Kent BR3 1AT
Croom Helm Australia Pty Ltd, Suite 4, 6th floor,
64-76 Kippax Street, Surry Hills, NSW 2010, Australia

British Library Cataloguing in Publication Data

John, F.A.
    Industrial product innovation: organisation
    and management.
    1. New products   2. Product management
    I. Title
    658.5'75   HD69.N4

    ISBN 0-7099-1444-X

First published in the United States of America 1985 by
Nichols Publishing Company, Post Office Box 96,
New York, NY 10024

Library of Congress Cataloging in Publication Data

Johne, F.A.
    Industrial product innovation.

    Bibliography: p.
    Includes index.
    1. Technological innovations.   2. New products.
I. Title.
T173.8.J64   1985   658.5'038   85-13580
ISBN 0-89397-233-9

Printed and bound in Great Britain

CONTENTS

LIST OF TABLES

ABBREVIATIONS USED

ATE	Automatic Test Equipment
BSI	British Standards Institution
BU	Business Unit (also referred to as SBU)
CAD	Computer Aided Design
CEO	Chief Executive Officer
COO	Chief Operating Officer
DIN	German Industry Norm or Standard
DOI	Department of Industry
DMM	Digital Multimeter
DVM	Digital Voltmeter
ESRC	Economic and Social Research Council
GM	General Manager
IEEE	Institution of Electrical and Electronic Engineers
LSI	Large Scale Integration
MD	Managing Director
MoD	Ministry of Defence
MPU	Microprocessor Unit
PERA	Production Engineering Research Association
R&D	Research and Development (also Engineering)
ROI	Return on Investment
RMS	Root Mean Squared
SIMA	Scientific Instruments Manufacturers' Association
SBU	Strategic Business Unit
T&M	Test and Measurement
ULA	Uncommitted Logic Array
QA	Quality Assurance
VP	Vice-President

PREFACE

This book has been written for both
practitioners and for students of industrial
organisation, marketing and engineering. Product
innovation, that is to say the development of new
products, lies at the heart of competitive activity
in all firms experiencing rapid changes in
technology and in their markets. In such circumstances a firm can either stand still and risk
being overtaken by events, or it can seek to be
among the leaders of change by offering to customers
improved products for which a premium price can
frequently be charged.

The detailed case investigations of current
practice contained in this book result from a study
of product innovation in one high technology
manufacturing industry - the electrical and
electronic test and measurement instrument industry.
In this industry product innovation is of critical
importance for competitive purposes and many
examples are provided of how skilled handling of the
tasks involved can safeguard the future of a firm in
times of rapid technological and market changes.

The book highlights current organisational practices in two main types of firms. The first group
is composed of active and experienced product
innovator firms which are referred to as 'innovative
firms'. The organisational practices of three
innovative firms are analysed and contrasted with
those of three less active and experienced product
innovator firms. The latter are referred to in the
book as 'less innovative firms'.

A special feature of the book is to alert the
reader to limitations in considering only formal

organisational structures, because these often reflect solely the latest fashion in management practice. For example, it is shown that whilst new product committees are found in both innovative and also in less innovative firms, some firms use such structural devices in ways which give surprisingly better results. To assist in interpreting real rather than superficial differences in organisational structuring the reader is provided with a framework with which each of the case investigations in the book can be interpreted. The framework will also be found useful for interpreting the organisation structures of firms in a wide range of other manufacturing industries.

Because product innovation is becoming increasingly important in manufacturing industry the book will appeal especially to persons in firms which are not as yet active and experienced in this particular area of competitive activity. Undergraduate and postgraduate students of business studies and engineering will find that the introductory chapters and the supporting case material provides up to date examples of current industrial marketing practices in US and British manufacturing firms.

ACKNOWLEDGEMENTS

The greatest debt which an author of a serious book owes is usually to those who provide him with relevant facts from which he can develop and test a set of propositions which underpin his main arguments. And so it is with this book, which would not have been possible without the willing help of many busy executives in manufacturing firms who generously shared their time and ideas with me. To respect confidences their names are not mentioned.

Financial assistance to carry out an extensive set of field interviews in Britain and the US was provided by the Economic and Social Research Council, London. I would also like to acknowledge with grateful thanks the help and support given to me by my colleagues at the City University Business School, London.

Chapter One

THE IMPORTANCE OF PRODUCT INNOVATION

It is commonly believed that nearly 90% of new products launched by firms fail to fulfil commercial objectives. However, recent research carried out by Crawford (1979), Hopkins (1981) and Cooper (1982, 1983) in the US points to an average failure rate for industrial products of only about 35%. The results of these recent research studies represent an important discovery because they indicate that industrial firms as a whole have become considerably better at developing new products than was previously thought.

What is of even greater importance is that almost all recent research into product innovation has stressed that there is wide variation around the average failure rate, which implies that some firms are now much better at developing new products than are others. Indeed, it was this phenomenon which provided the initial stimulus for undertaking the study on which this book is based. The design features and principal findings of that study are described in Chapter 4 which outlines the background to the case investigations which make up the bulk of this book. The purpose of the study was to find out whether firms which are experienced at developing new products organise themselves in a way which is different from that of less experienced firms. Suffice it to say, by way of introduction, that important differences were found in the way experienced product innovators organise. These differences include not only the way product innovation is formally organised, but more importantly, the way specialist tasks are actually performed, informally as it were, by those involved in developing new products.

The organisational practices of six firms are considered in detail in this book. Three of the firms are active and experienced product innovators and three are less active product innovators. The organisational systems of each firm are described in detail, often in the words of managers working within them. All the firms manufacture and market electrical and electronic test and measuring equipment, such as analogue and digital voltmeters; ammeters; multimeters; oscilloscopes; spectrum and logic analysers, which are sold to a wide range of industrial end - user markets. The instrument manufacturing industry was selected for study because it contains some of the world's most active product innovator firms which have gone a long way to develop into a very fine art the tasks involved in successfully bringing new products to market.

The organisational practices of three experienced product innovator firms are described in Chapter 5. These are contrasted, in Chapter 6, with those of firms with less experience of the tasks involved. The three experienced firms are acknowledged leaders in product innovation in the instrument industry with a long and successful record of introducing new products on to the market. This is not to say that they have never suffered a new product failure. They probably all have; however, what singles them out for special attention is the fact that they have learned, through regular and disciplined product innovation, to overcome many of the problems associated with failure.

Managers in manufacturing industry will have no difficulty in relating to the material in each of the cases described in Chapters 5 and 6. Those managers who work in firms which are already pursuing an active product innovation policy will find the practices of the three experienced firms of particular interest. This is because there is much to learn from the best performers in an industry, such as instrument manufacturing, in which regular product innovation is an essential ingredient of sustained business performance. Managers at present working in firms with little or no experience of product innovation will find much to relate to in the case investigations contained in Chapter 6, because particular emphasis is placed on identifying how product innovation might be stimulated in them.

Before reading the cases all readers are strongly recommended to look at Chapters 2 and 3 at least. This is because these two preliminary chapters provide the key to interpreting the narrative material contained in the case investigations

THE ROLE OF PRODUCT INNOVATION

Product innovation, that is to say, the development and launching of new products, is one of the most important tasks in manufacturing firms which compete in fast-changing markets and technological environments. Product innovation is particularly challenging for firms which are applying the latest advances in technology. Yet, despite its importance, product innovation cannot, on its own, be expected to guarantee business success in manufacturing firms. Competitive success results from pursuing an appropriate amalgam of different types of innovation. Whilst Ansoff (1965) stressed the importance of technological and marketing innovation (see Table 1.1) it is important to remember that a firm needs to concern itself also with other important types of innovation - innovation in its financial systems; innovation in its personnel and industrial relations practices; innovation in its purchasing practices - all of which can contribute to profitable business growth.
A glance at Table 1.1 shows that product innovation is a variant of technological innovation. The aim of product innovation is to offer customers radically new or incrementally improved new products based on technological advances. It will be noticed that another important variant of technological innovation is process innovation. The aim of technological process innovation is to reduce the costs of manufacturing existing products. Whilst both technological product and process innovation are important to manufacturing firms, product innovation is arguably the most important in the long run because it can ensure survival in times of rapid changes in technology and markets. For, no matter how skilled marketing personnel might be in penetrating existing markets more efficiently or in developing new markets for old products, and how much manufacturing costs can be reduced through process innovation, the time will come when existing products will have served their purposes. Without

3

new products to replace old ones a manufacturing firm will ultimately wither and die.

THE NATURE OF PRODUCT INNOVATION

Product innovation is made possible through invention. A radically new product typically incorporates one or more recent technological inventions. The process of commercially exploiting such inventions is referred to as innovation. Incremental product innovation is concerned, broadly speaking, with the commercial exploitation of less advanced technology.

TABLE 1.1

<u>ANSOFF'S GROWTH VECTOR MODEL</u>

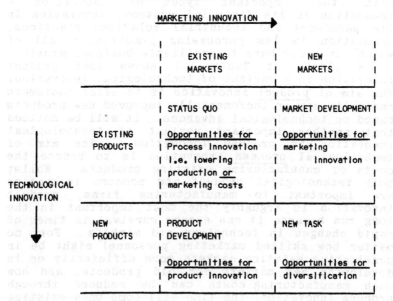

SOURCE : Ansoff (1965 : 99)

It is important to note that the categorisation of innovation as "radical" or as "incremental" depends entirely on the background of those involved in applying a technological advance for commercial purposes. For example, the invention of the microprocessor unit provided manufacturers of advanced electronic products with an opportunity for "incremental" product innovation. For these manufacturers the microprocessor presented a useful step up from the less versatile silicon chip. However, the same invention offered manufacturers of less advanced electrical products the opportunity for "radical" product innovation, because they had not used sophisticated micro-electronic components before.

It has already been mentioned that both technological product and process innovation are important to manufacturing firms operating in fast-changing environments. This poses businessmen with the problem of how to strike a balance between these two types of innovation. In this connection the analytical assertions of Utterback (1979) provide useful insight into the issues involved:

> The stimulus for innovation changes as a [manufacturing] unit matures .... Uncertainty about markets and appropriate targets is reduced as the unit develops, and larger research and development investments are justified. At some point, before the increasing specialization of the unit makes the cost of implementing technological innovations prohibitively high and before increasing price competition erodes profits with which to fund large indirect expenses, the benefits of research and development efforts reach a maximum ...... A strong commitment to research and development is characteristic of productive units in the middle stages of development. Such units invest heavily in formal research and engineering departments, with emphasis on process innovation and product different- iation through functional improvements. ....Units in different stages of evolution ... undertake different types of innovation.

Utterback's assertions are important because they suggest the existence of two distinct cycles of

The Importance of Product Innovation

technological innovation within manufacturing firms:
one reflecting the rate of product innovation, the
other the rate of process innovation. Table 1.2
illustrates these generalised assertions, which are
based on the assumption that younger firms will have
a greater proportion of new products in their
portfolio than older firms.

TABLE 1.2

DIFFERENT TYPES OF TECHNOLOGICAL INNOVATION

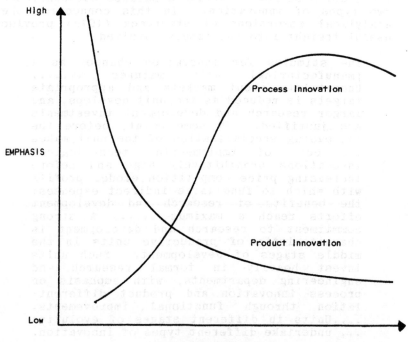

SOURCE : Adapted from Utterback & Abernathy (1975 : 645)

6

WHY FIRMS INNOVATE AT DIFFERENT RATES

As far as the rate of technological innovation is concerned there is now considerabe evidence which points to the pervading influence of competitive pressure. Empirical research by Townsend et al. (1981) in the UK, and by von Hippel (1978, 1982) in the US, has shown that the most frequent form of technological innovation - incremental product innovation - occurs as a result of applying inventions made outside a firm. Already in 1962 Schumpeter referred to a "gale of creative destruction" when the communality of inter-firm competition is broken from outside and the survival of those firms unable or unwilling to innovate is threatened. On the other hand, when inter-firm competition is not strong, and when barriers to entry are high, considerable delays can occur.
When competitive pressure is high it will undoubtedly be necessary for a firm involved in manufacturing advanced technology products to engage in both product and process innovation. By engaging in technological product innovation a firm can usually charge a premium price for specially developed features. Later, as competitors follow the leaders emphasis moves to technological process innovation, that is to say, manufacturing at the lowest possible unit cost. Both types of technological innovation rely on engineering (Research & Development) input, and, as has been well put by Steele (1975):

> Out of such new directions comes the self-renewal that maintains the vitality and viability crucial to large corporations if they are to continue to warrant their birthright.

However, as has been stressed by many analysts, there is no universally accepted method for measuring particular innovative activities which contribute to the quality, efficiency and costs of industrial products. To engage in too much R&D is wasteful of the firm's resources. To engage in too little, in the hope of selling existing products in new markets (see Table 1.1), can only be a short-term solution. In the longer-term a firm which seeks to manufacture and market higher technology

products will need to invest in R&D expenditure or
accept that its products and processes will be
overtaken by competitors either from inside the
industry or from outside it.

Whilst competitive pressure can act as a spur to
technological innovation it is, on its own,
insufficient to explain differences in the type and
degree of innovation pursued by particular firms.
Why is it, for example, that firms such as Hewlett-
Packard or 3M consistently lead the competition in
many product markets, whilst other firms follow?
Here recent work in the business policy area
provides considerable insight. Writers such as
Steiner (1979), Porter (1980), and Ansoff (1984) all
conceive a firm's strategy as the starting point of
the management process. They argue that technological innovation will be pursued by a firm as a
result of a will or a 'strategy' as they call it.
If there is no will to innovate, with any sense of
urgency, then outside competitive pressure, or even
having the necessary resources, will not be
sufficient to make things happen.

DIFFERENT TYPES OF INNOVATOR FIRMS

Accepting that different strategies are pursued
by firms as far as product innovation is concerned
one is faced with the problem of how to classify
these strategies. Freeman (1974) has explained the
phenomenon whereby some firms regularly lead in
terms of technological product innovation by
suggesting that such strategies are "offensive",
whilst those of followers are "defensive". Miles &
Snow (1978) in addressing the same phenomenon speak
of "prospector" firms and of "reactor" firms, whilst
Miller & Friesen (1982) speak of "entrepreneurial"
and of "conservative" firms.

A most useful rationale for understanding
differences in the pace of technological innovation
on the part of manufacturing firms has been provided
by Ansoff et al. (1976) and by Nystrom (1979) who
conceive firms as operating, at any one point in
time, in either the "entrepreneurial" mode or in the
"positional" mode. Firms in the entrepreneurial
mode are concerned with change, whilst those in the
positional mode are concerned with maintaining the
status quo, particularly as far as their product
range is concerned.

8

Whilst it is common practice for firms to pursue strategies which are appropriate to particular products and/or markets, it is also true that some firms in an industry are commonly regarded as more active product innovators than others. This phenomenon is particularly pronounced in those product markets in which certain firms have built up for themselves a reputation for regularly leading in the introduction of new products, whilst others follow their lead.

The major product innovation strategies open to a firm in relation to a particular product market are shown in Table 1.3. The table suggests active product innovator firms move ahead either on a broad front or on a narrower one. Less innovative firms, on the other hand, will either react to competitive pressure or defend existing products. In the case investigations which follow in Chapters 5 and 6 each firm's current product innovation strategy has been assessed in accordance with the schema depicted in Table 1.3 in relation to the stand-alone instrument product market.

TABLE 1.3

DIFFERENT PRODUCT INNOVATION STRATEGIES

THE INNOVATIVE FIRMS	THE LESS INNOVATIVE FIRMS
Broad span product innovators Such firms lead by introducing new products into several related product market segments	**Reactors** Such firms introduce new products in response to competitive pressure
Narrow span product innovators Such firms lead by introducing new products into particular market segments	**Defenders** Such firms safeguard existing products mainly by process innovation i.e. cutting manufacturing costs

The Importance of Product Innovation

SUMMARY

In this introductory chapter the nature and causes of product innovation have been discussed and its importance to firms operating in fast-changing technological and market environments has been stressed. It was shown that whilst various product innovation strategies are open to firms these can be categorised into two main types - innovative and less innovative. It was argued that as a general rule it is active and experienced product innovator firms which pursue proactive strategies whilst reactive strategies are pursued by firms which are less active and therefore have less experience of product innovation. It is this two-fold categorisation which provides the rationale for the exposition of the case material in this book in which the organisational mechanisms used by innovative firms in Chapter 5 are compared with those in less innovative firms in Chapter 6.

Chapter Two

PRINCIPAL ORGANISATIONAL DESIGNS

Before reviewing the span of possible
organisational designs it is important to reflect on
the different types of product innovation which a
firm can engage in. Broadly speaking there are two
types: (1) radical product innovation, and (2)
incremental product innovation. Radical product
innovation involves using advances in technology to
offer customers a new line of products. Incremental
product innovation involves using existing
technology to extend an established product line or
to improve product performance to a certain degree.
These two types also describe the extent of
technical risk, for clearly there is likely to be a
higher technical risk involved in launching a new
product line than there is in the case of a product
improvement. However, as is shown in Table 2.1
higher technical risk can be compounded by higher
market risk, as for example when a firm decides to
sell a new product line in a completely new market.

Table 2.1
MAIN TYPES OF PRODUCT INNOVATION

	Market(s) known to the firm	Market(s) new to the firm
Using new "state of the art" technology	(1) RADICAL PRODUCT INNOVATION	e.g. a new product line
Using existing technology	(2) INCREMENTAL PRODUCT INNOVATION	e.g. an extension to a product line or product improvements

11

CENTRALISED/DECENTRALISED CONTROL

Because of the high risk associated with radical product innovation in particular, a major decision to be made by top management is how far to delegate authority for this away from the corporate centre. The issue is particularly challenging in multi-divisionalised firms, which is why these are used as examples to describe the span of possible organisation structures.

In practice the degree to which top management decides to delegate authority for product innovation is likely to depend very much on the circumstances facing a firm. For example, the very size of a firm can influence this decision, because it is often necessary to delegate authority to several tiers of management in large firms to avoid overloading top officers. Similarly, the type of markets in which a firm sells and the type of technology it is using are both likely to determine the extent to which it is possible to control developments satisfactorily from the centre. Complex and fast-changing markets or technology will almost certainly demand that many decisions are taken where the action is most fierce (i.e. at the divisional level) rather than at the corporate level. The quality of the firm's personnel will also influence how far it is possible to delegate authority, because the staff of some firms lack the skills required to control and coordinate product innovation without direction from the centre.

The decision whether or not to centralise or decentralise product innovation in a firm is, additionally, likely to be influenced by the type of organisational mechanisms with which the firm has historically felt happy. A choice needs to be made on the degree of permanence given to particular organisational arrangements. A glance at Table 2.5 will reveal that Divisions, Departments, Groups and Standing Committees are features of permanent organisational arrangements. On the other hand, Task Forces or Project Teams are temporary organisational mechanisms which are established to deal with particular problems and disbanded thereafter.

Permanent organisational mechanisms are used by all firms of a size which requires separate functional specialisation. Temporary organisational mechanisms are more recent devices, and for this reason are as yet less widely used. Indeed, task forces or project teams are regarded with some scepticism by the top management of many firms, particularly those which have little or no experience of using result-related, as opposed to input-related, organisational mechanisms. For example, in a survey of product innovation in UK firms, Randall (1980) found that only half the firms had ever used project teams.

Last, but almost certainly not least, organisation design is frequently influenced not only by the need to fit certain operational circumstances, but also by fashion. In this connection the case investigations in Chapter 5 provide a useful insight into how the management philosophies and organisational practices of certain experienced product innovator firms have diffused among the wider population of instrument manufacturers.

Advantages of Centralised Control

An example of centralised control of product innovation is shown in Table 2.2. The main advantages of this organisational arrangement are as follows:

* It can ensure coordination aimed at developing products which are in the best interests of the company as a whole and not just of a division.
* It can avoid duplication of effort in various divisions of a company.
* It can be used to retain direct control over very expensive and risky new product developments.
* It can be used to stimulate and control radical product innovation, particularly that associated with conglomerate diversification; that is to say, when a firm seeks to enter a completely new product market which is not served by an existing division.

Table 2.2

CENTRALISED CONTROL OF PRODUCT INNOVATION

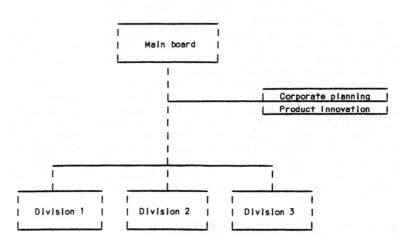

Advantages of Decentralised Control

Decentralised control over product innovation is designed to overcome the major disadvantage accompanying centralised control which has to do with lack of initial involvement of divisions which will ultimately have to manage the new product. This lack of initial involvement can lead to a loss of commitment on the part of persons in a division. Table 2.3 illustrates the salient features of decentralised control of product innovation. The specific operational advantages of this form of organisational arrangement are as follows:

* New products are likely to be attuned closely to a division's technological capabilities, as well as to its market strengths and opportunities. This can increase the chances of commercial success.
* It is probably the most effective way of controlling product innovation in a conglomerate firm, where each division has substantially different products lines, uses different technologies and sells to different market segments.

14

* Most important, it places authority for product innovation where the action is, and where the results will be readily measurable. At this level there is likely to be considerable commitment on the part of staff to exploiting ideas for new products in which the future prosperity of the division lies.
* It may result, consequently, in more and better ideas for new products. The development of these ideas into tangible products can be expedited because of shorter lines of communication between divisional marketing, engineering (R&D) and manufacturing personnel.

Table 2.3

DECENTRALISED CONTROL OF PRODUCT INNOVATION

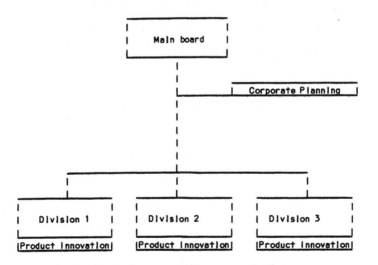

Advantages of Dual Control

A major potential disadvantage accompanying decentralised control of product innovation is that divisions may only undertake pedestrian, relatively low-risk product improvements. In order to control

for this possibility, and also to check that there
is no unnecessary duplication in development efforts
across divisions, some companies have introduced
dual control as is shown in Table 2.4. Despite the
fact that this form of organisational arrangement
splits responsibilities, and therefore requires more
staff for communication purposes, it offers the
following potential advantages:

* The corporate centre can handle radical
  product innovation, that is to say, high budget; high technical risk; high market risk
  projects, whilst incremental product innovation is handled at the divisional level.
* Provides an organisational mechanism for
  allocating company-wide resources where they
  are likely to be most productive.
* Helps to engender an innovative atmosphere
  throughout the whole firm.
* The corporate level concentrates on stimulating business opportunities which might lead
  to the establishment of new divisions.
* The corporate level coordinates basic
  technical and market research which might
  stimulate and assist product innovation in
  several different divisions.

Table 2.4

DUAL CONTROL OF PRODUCT INNOVATION

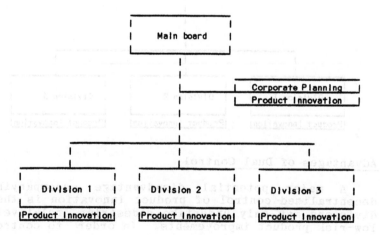

16

PRINCIPAL DESIGNS

The span of organisational designs discussed in this chapter is listed in table 2.5. The first two designs - New Venture Departments and New Venture Teams - have as their primary aim the pursuit of radical product innovation at the corporate level. All the other designs are used primarily for incremental product innovation, at either the corporate level, or the divisional level. As in the previous section, emphasis is placed on identifying important advantages resulting from the use of particular devices. The last part of the chapter deals with the potential advantages and disadvantages of using an amalgam of organisational devices.

Designs Suited for Radical Product Innovation

1.1 New Venture Group or Department

There can be no doubt that product innovation is disruptive of the on-going activities of a firm. For example, production systems may have to be altered to accommodate new products; selling skills may have to be augmented to promote new products; development funds will need to be spent on speculative ventures, as opposed to less risky process innovation. Indeed, sometimes a firm may be so locked into manufacturing and marketing its existing products that there is little or no expertise for product innovation. In such circumstances, because very few persons can be looked upon to suggest, let alone to develop new products of any real technological sophistication, the firm may decide to establish a New Venture Group or Department which is completely separate from its present on-going manufacturing and commercial activities.

Fast (1978) has shown that New Venture Groups or Departments were originally intended to be permanent centralised organisational devices outside the normal operating structure of the firm. Their prime purpose being conglomerate diversification, that is to say, diversification into business activities different from the firm's current manufacturing and

17

marketing operations. An essential feature of such Groups and Departments was that they aimed at diversification by internal business efforts rather than by means of external acquisition.

Table 2.5

PRINCIPAL ORGANISATIONAL DESIGNS

DESIGNS SUITED FOR RADICAL PRODUCT INNOVATION:

Permanent	Temporary
1.1 New Venture Group or Department	1.2 New Venture Team

DESIGNS SUITED FOR INCREMENTAL PRODUCT INNOVATION:

Permanent	Temporary
2.1 Standing New Product Committee	2.2 Temporary New Product Committee
3.1 New Product Department (Staff)	
3.2 New Products Department	
3.3 Marketing Department	
3.4 Technical Department	3.5 Marketing Department led Project Team
	3.6 Technical Department led Project Team
	3.7 Inter-Departmental Project Team
4.	Modular Matrix

18

Usually a New Venture Group or Department was tightly structured and received explicit instructions from top management on the type of business operation the firm was to enter - in terms of markets and technology. Members joined the Group or Department permanently. Their responsibility was to develop a new business to such a stage that it is ready to be established as a separate division or SBU.

The arguments for setting up New Venture Groups or Departments rest on three main assumptions. First, that it is necessary to create a centre of responsibility for new business development to ensure that this activity receives sufficient attention. Second, to provide the organisational climate and structure appropriate for new business development. Third, to insulate new business development activities from the dominant values and norms of the parent firm. The rationale has been well described by Drucker (1974:799) as follows:

> The search for innovation needs to be organized separately and outside of the on-going managerial business. Innovative organizations realize that one can not simultaneously create the new and take care of what one already has. They realize that maintenance of the present business is far too big a task for the people in it to have much time for creating the new, the different business for tomorrow...... Innovative organizations, therefore, put the new into separate organizational components concerned with the creation of the new.

The New Venture Group or Department approach to launching new business activities was widely adopted by larger firms in the 1960s and early 1970s. Fast (1979:266) has made the important distinction between macro groups, such as have been discussed so far, and micro teams which are temporary organisational devices with a more limited charter, which are discussed below. Macro New Venture Groups or Departments were, in their heyday, given a high profile because there was an expectation that they would revitalise or redirect the firm. Unfortunately for them, their life was relatively short-lived, as has been shown by a number of analysts (Dunn 1977; Fast,1978), because when the corporate strategic situation changed the Group was no longer needed, and as the Group's political position eroded it came to be rejected by the power structure. Other reasons for the demise of New Venture Groups or Departments are:

* Costs in terms of staffing and budgets because the Groups or Departments were intended to be self-supporting and separate from on-going corporate activities.
* Over time some groups became institutionalised and so lost their innovative edge.
* The realisation in firms that product innovation should be a continuous process with which ideally nearly all personnel should be involved rather than a select few.

Fast (1978:84) has even gone so far as to assert that in most firms New Venture Groups or Departments represent a misfit because they are neither a staff department nor an operating division, but a hybrid of the two. He claims: "Because of this peculiar identity, it exists in a state of disequilibrium. It tends to have a relatively short life span (approximately four to five years) and to become inoperative by evolving...". What Fast suggests is that once a New Venture Group has successfully created a new business, its job is done, and it may become a smaller staff department advising on new products, or it may be disbanded altogether.

1.2 New Venture Team

It has now become quite widely accepted that firms are likely to be more successful in diversification efforts which are in areas closely related to their existing business, that is to say, concentric diversification which is more focussed and less costly. Many firms which have passed through the stage of having established a New Venture Group or Department now place emphasis on more restricted new venture charters, less autonomous methods of operation and the involvement of staff who keep a lower profile in the firm (Dunn, 1977).

Some analysts have argued that venture team management furnishes a temporary team of specialists

20

with freedom to develop a new business. Sands
(1983) points out that such a venture team (or Micro
New Venture Group, as Fast has called it) is created
with freedom to carry through a mini diversification
project, and that if the new venture succeeds the
team may be spun off as a separate division or SBU.
The team is not, however, expected to make a major
impact in terms of redirecting the firm's business
mission. Indeed, this mechanism is frequently used
to-day as a means for retaining internal
entrepreneurs, or product champions, who do not fit
in readily with existing organisational
arrangements.

Whilst a New Venture Team's composition is
clearly less grandiose than that of a New Venture
Group or Department it is more stable than that of a
task force (described later). Midgley (1977:197)
points out that a New Venture Team frequently comes
into existence after the idea generation and initial
screening stages which may have been carried out by
staff specialists. Assignment to a New Venture Team
has been described by King (1973)as a considerable
opportunity in as much as "the venture manager of
today becomes the divisional manager of tomorrow".
Similarly, other members of the New Venture Team may
become the top management of a new division or SBU.
Fast (1979) sees the primary role of a New Venture
Team as efficiency in new business development by
maximising the proportion of successful ventures,
whilst minimising their cost. Typically, he argues,
they launch beach-head type ventures built on a
single product aimed at a small well-defined market
niche. The objective being to test the business
idea before making a major corporate commitment.

The specific advantages of New Venture Teams are:

*   They allow a firm to explore and develop a
    'next generation' product line outside the
    on-going operation which it would threaten if
    successful.
*   They provide concentrated inter-functional
    specialisation, which will allow progress to
    be made quickly, because it is not held back
    by existing job commitments.

The major problems with this organisational device
are: (i) the need to find qualified personnel who
are prepared, for a time, to leave the mainstream of

the firm's operations, (ii) excessive enthusiasm,
which may lead ventures to gain a momentum of their
own, and (iii) the assumption that if a firm has a
New Venture Team no one else need worry about
product innovation.

Designs Suited for Incremental Product Innovation

2.1 Standing New Product Committee

A Standing New Product Committee frequently
complements other organisational mechanisms charged
with product innovation for the explicit purpose of
encouraging, coordinating and controlling a firm's
new product efforts. In such cases membership
frequently consists of top-level marketing and
development (R&D) personnel, as well as the firm's
other senior officers. Table 2.6 illustrates the
place of a Standing New Product Committee in the
overall organisation and shows that it provides a
dual control over product innovation (as was
discussed earlier).

Table 2.6

COORDINATING ROLE OF A STANDING NEW PRODUCT COMMITTEE

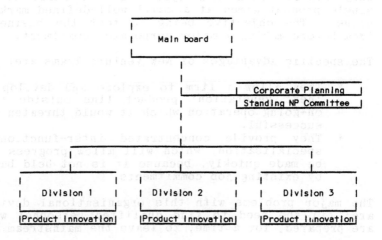

In a research study of product innovation in the UK Randall (1980: 11) found that most New Product Committees report to the MD or Chairman. He further found that 50% of medium sized and larger firms have such committees. Unfortunately, however, it is often difficult to discern whether a committee is a standing committee, as is being discussed here, or a temporary coordinating device (discussed below).

A Standing New Product Committee, as will be seen in some of the cases described in Chapter 5, can also be used to release initial sums of money to bright persons in a firm who wish to conduct a feasibility study into a possible new product opportunity. Such a feasibility study can complement on-going product innovation efforts in a division. When a New Product Committee acts in this way, its real strength lies in coordinating and controlling progress on individual product developments, particularly if it has the power to stop them at appropriate stages.

2.2 Temporary New Product Committee

Firms with little or no experience of product innovation sometimes establish a temporary committee, the express purpose of which is to explore product innovation opportunities. In such cases a senior corporate officer frequently acts as chairman over a cross-functional membership whose purpose is to initiate and progress individual product developments. This form of centralised organisational device has been much criticised because it shifts responsibility away from individuals and their existing business operations to a joint decision making body with shared responsibility. Hopkins (1974:47) quoted one organisation specialist as saying "Shared responsibilities too often mean responsibilities avoided". Whilst committees can serve as useful coordinating mechanisms, as was seen in the case of the Standing New Product Committee, their executive power is usually very limited, as will be seen in several of the cases described in Chapter 6.

3.1 New Product Department (Staff)

Whilst the New Venture Group or Department is a highly centralised organisational device aimed at

effecting radical product change, a less extreme
mechanism is the New Product Department (Staff), the
explicit task of which is to develop new products
which can later be taken up by constituent parts of
the firm. As is shown in Table 2.7 a New Product
Department (Staff) reports direct to the CEO, either
of the whole firm or of an important constituent
such as a Division or a SBU. Essentially, the
purpose of such a staff department is to assist the
CEO in spotting opportunities for new products and
to do something about exploiting the most
appropriate opportunities. When the firm
manufactures products based on higher technology the
department will not normally be able to undertake
expensive development work (in the way a New Venture
Team can) - hence its key contribution is in helping
the CEO to plan to introduce new products based on
the efforts of the line departments. Frequently,
New Product (Staff) Departments are headed up by a
Director or Vice-President of Innovation.

Table 2.7

NEW PRODUCT DEPARTMENT (STAFF)

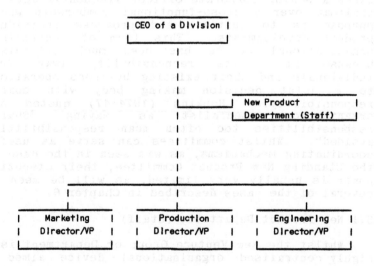

The success of a New Product Department (Staff) will depend almost entirely on the support given to it by the CEO (just as in the case of New Venture Groups or Teams). It is, after all, one thing to plan and to make recommendations on the sort of new products to be developed, but quite another to ensure that action is taken by the functional departments concerned - marketing, engineering (R&D) and manufacturing. Even when recommendations are developed into technically feasible new products, the line departments will always have a ready excuse if a new product subsequently fails commercially - after all, the new product wasn't their idea in the first place!

3.2 New Products Department

A New Products Department, if it is a line department, will be on the same lateral level as other functions in the firm, as is shown in Table 2.8. With such an organisational device responsibility for the development of new products is clearly ascribed to this one department. Watton (1969) has described the advantages as follows:

> First, the use of a new-products department clarifies and delineates responsibility in the company for new-product development. If responsibility is placed with the marketing, R&D, engineering, or market research departments, for example, new-product development usually becomes a part-time or secondary goal of that department. When responsibility is placed with the new-products department, innovation becomes a full-time concern and primary goal.

This option has been described as a sensible choice when a firm has the resources to sustain a large and continuing new products programme and also when new items are unrelated to existing products in the line, or where new products will move the firm into unfamiliar markets and technical areas (Hopkins, 1974:26). Having a separate New Products Department is generally considered least appropriate for incremental product innovations, which can be undertaken by existing business functions.

Table 2.8

NEW PRODUCTS DEPARTMENT

```
                    | Chief Executive |
                    |     Officer     |
                             |
                             |
                             |
                             |
  _____|_____
 |               |                  |                  |
 |               |                  |                  |
 |               |                  |                  |
 |               |                  |                  |
 | Marketing |   | Production |   | Engineering |   | New Products|
 | Director/VP |  | Director/VP |  | Director/VP |   | Director/VP |
```

The specific advantages of this form of organisational device are:

* Clear-cut and undiluted responsibility for product innovation.
* Potentially a balanced approach without functional bias.
* High visibility can ensure management interest and attention, which can help with cooperation from functional departments.

Major problems with this organisational device are: (i) the department may become isolated, elitist and impractical, (ii) there is potential for friction when dealing with other functional departments, particularly when handing over new products after development.

3.3   Marketing Department

Some firms ascribe responsibility for product innovation to the marketing function on the assumption that it is the best suited for the task because of its overview of existing commercial activities. This organisational arrangement occurs most frequently in firms in which marketing is acknowledged to be the prime line function, as is the case in most fast-moving consumer goods manufacturing firms. Two main formats can be used:

(1)   New Product Group
    Under this organisational arrangement a number of persons is given special responsibility for product innovation. The advantage of the arrangement is that such persons are close to the market by virtue of their departmental allegiance. The potential disadvantage is that such persons lack a broad and balanced perspective, especially with regard to technical considerations. The biggest potential disadvantage of this organisational format is that there may be excessive emphasis on incremental product innovation and not enough attention given to radical product innovation.

(2)   New Product Manager
    If the firm manages the marketing of its existing products by using product managers it is possible to appoint additional new product managers. Under this system, as is shown in Table 2.9, product managers are responsible for the market performance of existing products, while new product managers are responsible for initiating, planning and coordinating efforts aimed at new products. This system for managing product innovation is to be found in many fast-moving consumer goods companies.

    In a study of 100 new product projects Souder (1978) found the new product manager system the second most frequently used organisational design. He commented, however, that the device cannot be regarded as highly effective because many projects handled in this way fail because the product did not perform adequately, which he ascribed to poor communication and poor collaboration between R&D and marketing. He observed:

    In short, there was little or no interface between R&D and marketing. In several cases the vice-president of marketing attempted to obtain technical assistance by going through the vice-president of R&D. But the long chain of command and involvement of so many people filtered the information, delayed response times and generally sapped the enthusiasm of the personnel. Lower level personnel did not feel that they could deal direct with each other.....

Table 2.9

NEW PRODUCT MANAGER SYSTEM

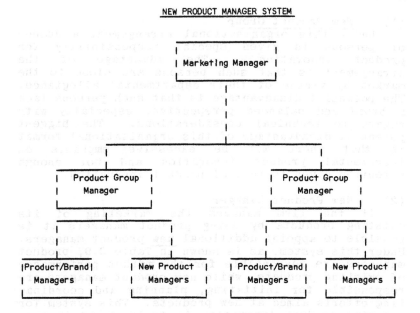

The new product manager system is undoubtedly a useful organisational device when product technology is well-understood and developed, but then, primarily for the purpose of effecting incremental product innovation.

3.4   Technical Department

The greatest advantages of locating responsibility for product innovation in a technical department is that new products are likely to be innovative in a technical sense. Also, it is likely to make efficient use of existing manufacturing facilities and technical back-up capabilities. Additionally, the creativity and productivity of R&D personnel can be stimulated.

The greatest potential disadvantages of ascribing responsibility for product innovation to solely a technical department is that there may be insufficient awareness of market needs. Secondly, there can be a tendency to spend time on developing 'technically-fascinating' products which result in protracted development times. King (1973:42) has expressed the problem well:

> Members of the R&D department are not inclined to start with the consumer and do not usually develop much skill in understanding consumer research. They tend to be further than most from the chief executive, who either regards them as backroom boffins or has an exaggerated respect for their technical knowledge. They tend to underestimate or even ignore the values of communication in a new brand. They tend to be too departmentally committed to do a good job of coordination, particularly with outside services.

In the 100 projects studied by Souder (1978) only 5 used this method. None achieved commercial success because in every case R&D was unable to get the marketing department to accept the finished product. This illustrates the danger inherent in "technology push" product innovation, where the driving force is the perceived potential of the new technology. In these circumstances marketing's role is secondary, being important only after the product has been developed. The problem centres on not using the creative abilities of technical personnel in a way which best serves the firm. Unfortunately, inspired new product idea generators in a technical department can get obsessed with the cleverness of an idea and may push its development with little or no market information, in the belief that the market will begin to appreciate its technical merits later. As many firms have found to their cost, this is really trying to sell a technical answer without being clear on what solution it is going to address.

3.5   Marketing Department led Project Team.

Project teams, which are sometimes also referred to as task forces are temporary ad hoc arrangements to coordinate and manage one or more phases of the development of a new product. Essentially, a team operates outside the established organisational structure and because of this frequently reports to top management. It is important to remember that this type of organisational format can be used in

29

addition to the permanent structure. For example, it is not uncommon to establish project teams which report to a firm's Standing New Product Committee.

When a project team is led by marketing an individual whose home base is the marketing department is appointed to manage the team. Commonly he is given a budget for the entire project and the team is drawn from several departments, with team membership varying in skills and size as needs change during development. At completion of the project all team members normally return to their home base.

Souder (1978:301) found that in the successful projects he studied in the US all project managers were "legitimised" in a personal letter from top management to all the concerned parties. The tone of the letter generally made it clear that the project was important and urgent and that others were expected to cooperate with the project manager. In no case did top management become involved in any details on the projects studied, although they were given detailed and regular feedback. A "part-icipative ambience" characterised the successful projects. The managers of successful projects were described by others involved as "someone who gets right in here and works with us" or "a guy who can tell you a lot about the user". A typical profile of the project leader was that he was 30-40 years old and had spent 6-10 years in R&D or engineering; had some patents or other technical achievements to his credit, and had spent 4-10 years in various marketing functions other than sales.

3.6 Technical Department led Project Team.

Technical departments are frequently organised to achieve specialisation in particular areas of expertise, for example metallurgy, electronics, instrumentation etc. Such designs are usually permanent and each member has a clear idea of his responsibilities, performance requirements and promotion prospects.

The problem with locating temporary project teams in technical departments is that it requires different managerial skills from those traditionally required in these departments. The problem is particularly acute because technologists frequently regard themselves primarily as professionals rather than as businessmen. Indeed, by training and natural inclination technologists often find it easier to relate to opposite numbers in other firms than to managers in other functions in their own firm. All these factors counsel caution in locating project teams in technical departments.

It is interesting to note that of the 100 projects studied by Souder (1978) - 50 successful and 50 unsuccessful - only two were managed by a Technical Department led Project Team. Both projects failed. In both cases marketing personnel did not feel sufficiently involved and so failed to contribute critical information. The projects did not stay on schedule and reports to top management were infrequent. Marketing department members of the project team lamented that R&D "was allowed to wander off". R&D personnel lamented that they received poor guidance and direction from marketing.

3.7 Inter-Departmental Project Team.

This organisational device is sometimes referred to as a "Dyad" because it normally always involves the two functions of marketing and R&D. An inter-departmental project team is frequently established by a firm's Standing New Product Committee (described in paragraph 2.1 above) to explore and later to develop particular new product opportunities. An excellent example of the way an inter-departmental project team can function effectively is illustrated in Chapter 5 in the John Fluke Manufacturing Company Inc. In this case the inter-departmental project team consisted of a formally appointed project leader who invited members of other functions to join the team as and when required. Throughout the life of the project the marketing and R&D functions were represented as a bare minimum. The project team met formally on a monthly basis and membership changed as the project metamorphosed over its life cycle.

The importance of effective teamwork in the development of successful new products, particularly between the marketing and technical functions, has been emphasised by many researchers (Souder 1978; Crawford 1979; Rothwell 1979; Hopkins 1981; Cooper 1982). Additionally, von Hippel (1978, 1982) and Parkinson (1982) have shown the importance of joint efforts with users in the successful development of new products. However, despite the clear advantages of inter-departmental project work, such an approach is undoubtedly difficult to manage, because it requires considerable skills. In particular, it requires skilful handling of the temperamental egos of inventive technical personnel whose efforts must be channelled, through interaction with marketing and other personnel, into doing not merely what is technically feasible, but also what is also commercially sound.

4. Modular Matrix.

The modular matrix approach to product innovation accepts the need for more than one type of organisational arrangement. Various permutations have been suggested and tried. Benson and Chasin (1976) proposed a new product management system comprising: (1) a new product development department, (2) an executive approval and review committee, (3) an ad hoc component including a task force or venture team, (4) a liaison committee, and (5) a new brand manager. Midgley (1977) proposed a somewhat simpler design comprising (1) staff specialists, (2) a new product review group, and (3) a venture team.

Fundamental to the modular matrix approach is the acceptance that permanent organisational mechanisms (such as a Standing New Product Committee) need to be augmented with temporary organisational mechanisms (such as Project Teams). The resulting matrix structure has been described well by Millman (1982) as follows:

> Matrix organisations evolved as a compromise between functional and project systems in an attempt to maintain the advantages of each. Projects requiring only small or sporadic input of expertise in a particular area can call upon the part-time services of a specialist instead of duplicating the employment of full-time persons for each project. This means that some specialists retain their reporting role to their functional manager whilst also having responsibility to a project manager.

The advantage of the team or project form of organisation is that it provides detailed control over separate functional tasks. This is precisely

32

what the functional organisation cannot provide, even when a committee has been established (because typically, such committees do not have executive power). Within specifically constituted project teams control may be further reinforced by invoking techniques (such as network analysis) to aid integration and to resolve conflicts which are likely to occur when representatives from different functions discuss a specific course of corporate action.

As is emphasised by Kolodny (1979:546) project management goes beyond conventional bureaucratic assumptions implicit in functional or classical management structures by (i) using horizontal coordination as well as vertical, (ii) providing in the form of project managers alternative authority figures to those with hierarchical power, (iii) focusing on tasks that are of limited duration and which are not conducive to the bureaucratic strengths of increasing efficiency through repetition and working down the learning curve, and (iv) delegating decisions downward to autonomous units rather than bucking them constantly up the hierarchy.

Certain larger multinational companies have taken the logic of matrix structures much further by using trilateral or even quadrilateral bases. In this way, resources are intergrated not only around products but also around geographical areas and markets. However, an attendant disadvantage of these new forms of organisational arrangements is that the position of managers can become ambiguous because within them a manager typically reports to multiple superiors, each with different priorities and pressures to impose. Accountability is not always clear, and as has been argued by Doyle (1979:326), "responsibilities are as unstable, transitory and ambiguous as the environments within which they operate."

As will be seen in Chapter 5 all active and experienced product innovator firms use some variant of the modular matrix, but make every effort to keep the arrangements as simple and easy to understand as possible. On the other hand, as will be seen in Chapter 6, such temporary organisational mechanisms have yet to find widespread acceptance for this purpose in less experienced product innovator firms. It will become evident in reading the cases that adopting a modular matrix approach to organising new product development can considerably facilitate the tasks involved.

SUMMARY

In this chapter the principal organisational devices which it is possible to use in firms for managing product development tasks were reviewed. The span of possible designs was summarised in Table 2.5. Most of the chapter concerned itself with the organisation of incremental product innovation, because this is the most common form of product innovation. It was emphasised that whilst all firms of a certain size will have a permanent organisation structure, efficiency in product innovation can be achieved by augmenting the permanent structure with temporary organisational devices such as project teams within a modular matrix structure.

Chapter Three

HIDDEN ORGANISATION STRUCTURES

The previous chapter considered the formal titles given to groups of persons involved in product innovation. An ever-attendant problem with formal titles is that these only give partial insight into the way work tasks are undertaken because different firms make different use of organisational devices such as Departments, Groups or Committees. This is so because persons operating within formal groupings are given or assume varying amounts of freedom to perform formally allocated responsibilities. One result is that it is simply not possible for formal titles to indicate in anything but bare outline how a particular grouping of people will actually perform its work. Some committees, for example, are very loosely structured and are run in a very participative way. Other committees, having nominally the same name, may be dominated by one or more persons inside or outside the committee structure or may be run in a very formal way.

Fortunately, sociologists have addressed this problem and have developed methods for identifying and measuring differences in the informal or "hidden" working structures of an organisation. For the purpose a number of different analytical approaches has been suggested. For example in the early part of the century Weber (1921/1947) popularised the notion of bureaucracy as an ideal way for conducting certain types of work. Much later Burns and Stalker (1961) suggested two principal ways for conducting work efficiently. They asserted that firms operating in fast-changing environments function best with an organic, that is to say, a loose, flexible and somewhat unclear formal organisation structure; whilst firms operating in a stable environment function best with a mechanistic, that is to say, a tightly controlled and clearly defined organisation structure.

Hidden Organisation Structures

An alternative approach, not based on hypothetical ideal structures, but aiming to measure the subtle and potentially important difference between one firm's structure and that of another is suggested in the work of Lawrence and Lorsch (1967). These two researchers postulated that a firm's operating structure can be measured with respect to the degrees of differentiation and integration achieved between separate functional departments. That is to say, according to the extent to which separate functions, such as Production, Sales, Research are different, yet integrated by means of effective communication.

Lawrence and Lorsch's approach was a useful step forward in attempting to capture what actually occurs within the formal organisation structure across the firm as a whole. However, for the purpose of measuring the ways in which firms differ in their approach to specific tasks (as opposed to broader functional departmental responsibilities), the analytical schemas developed in Britain by Pugh et al (1963) and in the US by Hage and Aiken (1970) provide extremely useful insights. These schemas are specifically designed to capture the essential elements of an organisation's informal or hidden structure.

Table 3.1

DIMENSIONS OF INFORMAL OR HIDDEN STRUCTURES

(I)   For structuring particular tasks:

SPECIALISATION - the degree of division of labour achieved internally in terms of functions and roles.

FORMALISATION - the extent to which rules, procedures and structures are written down for defining roles and for passing information.

STANDARDISATION - the degree to which roles are defined for carrying out tasks in a certain way, i.e. the consistency in reviewing related tasks and the frequency in doing so.

(II)   For coordinating and controlling the activities involved:

CENTRALISATION - the degree of dispersion of power by the chief executive officer (CEO).

STRATIFICATION - the degree that status differentials are adhered to in the execution of tasks.

36

Table 3.1 shows the five key dimensions identified in the work of Pugh et al. (1963) and Hage & Aiken (1970) for measuring how firms conduct their operations for the purpose of (i) undertaking particular tasks, and (ii) coordinating and controlling the activities involved.

For any particular task the five informal structural dimensions do, of course, need to be operationalised so as to embrace the specific activities involved. As far as product innovation is concerned there is now a rich body of literature which has identified key activities associated with developing new products successfully. These key activities have been listed in Table 3.2. Some are fairly self-evident, such as for example (3) Careful planning and control, and (4) Efficient development work. Others, however, are not so self-evident, particularly: (1) Good contact with the firm's market environment to determine accurately users' requirements, (2) Good internal co-operation and co-ordination between engineering (R&D), production and marketing, and (7) Existence of key individuals such as a product champion, a business innovator, a technical innovator etc.

Table 3.2

FACTORS UNDERLYING SUCCESS IN NEW PRODUCT DEVELOPMENT

1. Good contact with the firm's market environment to determine accurately users' requirements.

2. Good internal co-operation and co-ordination between engineering (R&D), production and marketing.

3. Careful planning and control.

4. Efficient development work.

5. The will on the part of top management to innovate.

6. Provision of good after-sales service and user education.

7. Existence of key individuals such as product champion, a business innovator, a technical innovator etc.

Source: Rothwell (1979); Hopkins (1981); Cooper (1982).

Hidden Organisation Structures

It is important to recognise that Table 3.2 does not represent a haphazard listing of activities which might be important in developing particular new products successfully. The list does, in fact, represent those activities which research has identified as being particularly important. There is now ample empirically based evidence which shows that falling down in any one of these activities is likely to lead to lack of success in developing a particular new product.

As is well-known to anyone with even just passing involvement in product innovation, the actual development process does not occur instantaneously. Usually, the process takes some considerable time - often several years - with normally more time being required for radical product innovations than for incremental product innovations. Ideally, during product development seven specific steps will be completed sequentially. Frequently, however, particularly in firms with less experience of product innovation, the necessary stages are performed simultaneously or on a recycling basis. The seven stages are shown in Table 3.3.

Table 3.3

MAIN PHASES IN THE PRODUCT INNOVATION PROCESS

INITIATION PHASE

(i)   Idea generation
(ii)   Screening out of unsuitable ideas
(iii)   Testing and development of suitable ideas in concept

EVALUATION PHASE

(iv)   Financial evaluation of alternative new product concepts

IMPLEMENTATION PHASE

(v)   Product development proper
(vi)   Test marketing
(vii) Launching

For the purpose of studying hidden organisation structures it is necessary to measure the activities involved in the two main phases of initiation and implementation. Indeed, the literature on organisational structuring strongly supports splitting the innovation process into these two main phases. For example, Zaltman et al. (1973); Baldridge & Burnham (1975); Dewar & Duncan (1977); Cummings & O'Connell (1978) have all argued that the initiation of innovation in an organisation is facilitated through a loose structuring of activities. And some of these writers have gone on to assert that for effective implementation a singleness of purpose is required, which can be achieved by a tight structuring of activities.

The assertions made in the organisation literature are especially interesting because they suggest that certain structures might be better suited for particular product innovation tasks. It follows that if this is found to be the case, certain organisations can be expected to display a shift in their hidden structure over the product innovation process. While the notion of a shift in a firm's hidden structures between initiation and implementation of product innovation may sound like a fanciful idea it is worth pointing out that the notion of such a shift in an organisation's task structures was explained well by Shepard as long ago as 1967. In an example of a military raiding unit operating in the Pacific during World War II, which made use of alternating organisational forms, he described how planning (initiation) was a joint activity involving the entire unit, with the private having as much opportunity to contribute as the colonel. However, during the execution (implementation) of a raid the same group operated under a strict and tightly controlled military command structure. More recently, the notion has been popularised by Peters & Waterman (1982) who have suggested that corporate performance can be aided by simultaneously loose-tight organisational structures.

Tables 3.4 and 3.5 show how the informal structural variables in Table 3.2 can be operationalised to embrace specific activities required in initiating and implementing product innovation. It was this set of questions which was used to collect information from all firms in the wider study described in the next chapter. Additionally, as will be seen in Chapters 5 and 6, all the case investigations include details on how individual firms were scored on each variable.

39

Hidden Organisation Structures

Table 3.4

HIDDEN STRUCTURES FOR INITIATING PRODUCT INNOVATION

1.1 Specialisation

(i) Do ideas for possible new products stem predominantly from one department, or do several departments involve themselves intimately in this task? (Functional specialisation)

    Low   ☐   One function only

                 ☐   Marketing and R&D

    High   ☐   Marketing, R&D and other(s)

(ii) By what means do those suggesting ideas get their inspiration? Are any specific activities engaged in – like brainstorming sessions – to increase the potential number of ideas? (Role specialisation)

    Low   ☐   Ad hoc

                 ☐   Ad hoc and analytical techniques
                      e.g. lost orders, exhibitions, market surveys

    High   ☐   Ad hoc and analytical techniques, and regular and
                      formal brainstorming, buzz sessions etc

1.2 Formalisation

(i) To what extent are those who involve themselves in suggesting ideas for possible new products given guidance or guidelines on this task in writing? (Written guidance)

    Low   ☐   Not at all

                 ☐   To some extent

    High   ☐   Extensively

(ii) To what extent is information on ideas for possible new products exchanged in writing between those involved? (Written communication)

    Low   ☐   Predominantly spoken

                 ☐   More spoken than written

    High   ☐   More written than spoken

1.3 Standardisation

(i) What guidance is given on the sort of new product ideas the company is seeking? (Consistency in control)

Low   ☐ Business mission delineated

       ☐ Product market area delineated

High   ☐ Product area delineated

(ii) How frequently are formal meetings held at which suggestions for possible new products are discussed? (Frequency of reviews)

Low   ☐ Less frequently than every 3 months

       ☐ At between 1 month and 3 monthly intervals

High   ☐ Monthly or more frequently

1.4 Centralisation

How much influence does the CEO exert over the flow of ideas for possible new products? (Power retention by CEO)

Low   ☐ He encourages as many ideas to be put forward as
         possible - the more the merrier

       ☐ He encourages ideas within the confines of the
         delineated strategy

High   ☐ He seeks to keep tight control over the sort of ideas
         which are put forward

1.5 Stratification

From what level in the organisation are ideas typically taken up? (Seniority of dominant coalition)

Low   ☐ Departmental executive level

       ☐ H O D level

High   ☐ Board level

41

Hidden Organisation Structures

Table 3.5

HIDDEN STRUCTURES FOR IMPLEMENTING PRODUCT INNOVATION

2.1 Specialisation

(I) Which department or departments are intimately involved in the development process? (Functional specialisation)

Low   ☐   R&D

         ☐   Marketing and R&D

High   ☐   Marketing, R&D and other(s)

(II) Certain types of activities can be particularly important in the development process. Do you, for example, have persons who assume responsibility for the following roles? (Role specialisation)

(1) Business/project management (i.e. product championship)
(2) Entrepreneurial interpretation of market trends (market gatekeeping)
(3) Analysis of scientific and engineering trends affecting the development (technical gatekeeping)
(4) Manufacturing/quality gatekeeping
(5) Godfathering (sponsorship by a senior member)

Low   ☐   2 or less roles are specifically provided for

         ☐   3-4 roles are specifically provided for

High   ☐   All roles are specifically provided for

2.2 Formalisation

(I) In what form are those involved in the development process given guidance or guidelines on their work? (Written guidance)

Low   ☐   The process is explained verbally

         ☐   Some written guidelines are given

High   ☐   A control manual is provided

(II) In what way is progress on specific development tasks noted? (Written communication)

Low   ☐   Informal notes are kept

         ☐   Formal notes are issued as required

High   ☐   Formal minutes of meetings are issued

HIDDEN STRUCTURES FOR IMPLEMENTING PRODUCT INNOVATION continued

2.3   Standardisation

(i)   Are the same development criteria applied to control each project? For example, has each project an equal chance of being stopped? (Consistency in control)

Low   ☐ Totally different criteria

         ☐ Somewhat different criteria

High   ☐ Essentially similar criteria

(ii)   How frequently is progress on development work monitored formally? (Frequency of reviews)

Low   ☐ Less frequently than every 3 months

         ☐ At between 1 month and 3 monthly intervals

High   ☐ Monthly or more frequently

2.4   Centralisation

What control or influence does the CEO exert over the development work? (Power retention by CEO)

Low   ☐ He expects others to get on with it independently

         ☐ He is kept in touch with progress

High   ☐ He is informed of progress in detail

2.5   Stratification

At what level is responsibility for the overall success of a project development assumed i.e. at whom is the finger pointed if something goes wrong? (Seniority of dominant coalition)

Low   ☐ Department executive level

         ☐ H O D level

High   ☐ Board level

SUMMARY

This chapter has explained a method for analysing the hidden operating structures used by firms in their endeavour to initiate and implement product innovation. These structures reflect the way work is actually undertaken rather than how it is intended to be undertaken. Two main categories of working structures were identified. First, those which reflect how particular activities are structured in terms of the amount of specialisation, formalisation and standardisation. Second, there are the structures which reflect how these activities are coordinated and controlled in terms of the amount of centralisation and stratification. It was shown how hidden structures can be measured in relation to the tasks involved in developing new products. These scales are used in Chapters 5 and 6 to measure variations in the informal structural arrangements used by particular firms.

Chapter Four

THE CONTEXT OF THE CASE INVESTIGATIONS

As was explained in Chapter 1 the case
investigations in Chapters 5 and 6 are drawn from a
wider study into the organisation of product
innovation in the instrument manufacturing industry.
The present chapter outlines the design, execution
and major findings of that study and so provides the
context of the cases which follow.

THE SAMPLE OF FIRMS

The sample of firms in the wider study was drawn
from the population manufacturing and marketing
electrical and electronic test, measurement and
control instruments in the UK under Standard
Industrial Classification (SIC) category 3442.
Instrument manufacturers were selected because this
industry contains some of the world's most active
industrial product innovator firms, which can be
expected, because of their accumulated experience,
to provide examples of best current practice. It
was decided to focus on a single manufacturing
industry to control for some of the contingencies
affecting operations - such factors as market
complexity and turbulence, as well as operating
technology, for example. It was also decided to
control for size, so that only firms with 100 or
more employees were included, to enable
investigation of interdepartmental interaction,
which is difficult to study in small firms.
A firm was defined as a manufacturing unit
trading in its own right - either as an independent
company, a division, or, as a business unit of a
holding company. However, even when firms are drawn
from a SIC four-figure industry classification there
can still be considerable diversity in their
operations. For example, some instrument firms have
much wider product ranges than others. To overcome

this problem the population was narrowed to include only firms manufacturing stand-alone instruments such as oscilloscopes, logic analysers, multimeters, digital voltmeters.

Instrument industry experts, who included manufacturers, persons selling components to these manufacturers, trade association personnel, users of stand-alone instruments in government, industry and the universities were asked for assistance in categorising firms into one of two groups. The first group comprising firms which are active and experienced product innovators; the second group firms which are not known for taking the initiative in product innovation.

The specific question asked of the industry experts was:

> Some firms are known to be more innovative than others in terms of offering customers new and improved products. In these firms, recently launched products account for a high proportion of total sales revenue. From your knowledge of the stand-alone test and measurement industry, which larger firms do you consider to be the most active and experienced in terms of launching new technologically based products?

The question was readily understood by industry experts because it referred to firms' activities in a particular product market. In consequence, the experts mentioned not merely the names of large multi-divisionalised companies such as Hewlett-Packard, Gould, G.E.C., Tektronix, but identified actual divisions or business units in these responsible for competing in the stand-alone test instrument market. In fact, eight firms were most frequently mentioned as having been active product innovators in the industry in recent years. Of these, four were US-owned, one was Dutch and three were British. These eight firms were then balanced out with a convenience sample comprising an equal number of British firms from the same industry which had not been mentioned as being active product innovators.

A semi-structured interview schedule was administered in face-to-face interviews with persons involved in product innovation tasks in the sample firms. Interviews were conducted between January

and December 1982 and each firm was visited on
several occasions to ensure that all relevant
personnel were interviewed. All firms agreed to
co-operate in the study, probably because
considerable care and preparation went into the
initial contact with each firm. First contact was
always made with the chief executive officer by
letter explaining the purpose of the study. On the
occasion of the first visit he, or his
representative, was asked to provide important
background information which is summarised for all
firms in Table 4.1. Thereafter directors, managers,
and project leaders/engineers were interviewed on a
"snowball" basis.

THE RESULTS

Important and statistically significant
differences in achievement were found between the
eight firms categorised by industry experts as being
innovative, that is to say, active and experienced
and the eight other firms. This is an interesting
result because it lends support to the research
approach used in the investigation. Specifically,
it was found that innovative firms rely far more on
recently introduced products for their sales
revenue. Not surprisingly, therefore, they claim
technological leadership for a higher percentage of
their product sales. They export a higher
proportion of sales and compete in markets which
have considerably higher growth rates than those
addressed by less innovative firms. The actual
differences between then two groups of firms are
shown in Table 4.1
    It is appropriate at this point to reiterate
that it was not the intention of the wider study to
demonstrate that the clear differences between the
eight innovative firms on the one hand, and the
eight less innovative firms on the other, are caused
directly by differences in their organisation
structures. The purpose of the study was confined
to showing why certain organisation structures might
be better suited for efficient product innovation.
However, it is not surprising, in our opinion, that
the structures identified as being best suited for
efficient product innovation are found predominantly
in firms which are active and experienced. After
all, such firms can be expected to have learned more
about structuring themselves to achieve desired
product innovation objectives.

The Context of the Cases

Table 4.1

<u>MAJOR DIFFERENCES BETWEEN THE TWO GROUPS OF FIRMS</u>

	INNOVATIVE FIRMS N = 8	LESS INNOVATIVE FIRMS N = 8
1. Percentage of current sales revenue accounted for by products introduced in the last 5 years	52% * (Range 80%-20%)	21% (Range 40%-5%)
2. Percentage of current sales revenue where the firm claims to have a clear technological lead with its products	52% (Range 80%-25%)	12% (Range 25%-0%)
3. Percentage of turnover being exported (1981/1982)	42% (Range 60%-18%)	12% (Range 25%-10%)
4. Current average annual growth rate of markets being addressed	20% (Range 40%-7%)	1% (Range 10%-neg.)
5. Percentage of turnover being spent on R&D (1981/1982)	13% (Range 16% - 6%)	3% (Range 5% - 1%)

* To be read as follows: Of the 8 innovative firms (in terms of product innovation) 52% of current sales came from products introduced in the last 5 years, within a range of 80% and 20% (an unweighted average is used).

SOURCE: Field interviews and secondary sources including inspection of certain company documents.

48

Formal Structures

All eight innovative firms were found to use
temporary project teams for managing product
innovation, whereas all eight less innovative firms
normally use permanent or semi-permanent new product
committees. The divide between the two groups could
not have been clearer as far as organisational
trappings are concerned. None of the innovative
firms possessed a permanent new product or venture
department, a finding which supports the critical
view propounded by Dunn (1977) that such departments
frequently fail to live long for reasons expressed
by one top corporate officer as follows: "If the
rest of the company perceives that members of the
venture group stand higher on the career-path
ladder, they will do their best to cut off the legs
of the venture group".
These findings suggest that all firms which
desire to emulate the example of active and
experienced product innovators should consider
establishing temporary project teams. That much is
likely to be easy, but it gives no guidance on how
project teams might optimally be managed.

Hidden Structures

To gain deeper insight into the complexities of
organisational decision making, particularly in
active and experienced product innovator firms, use
was made of the hidden structural measures which
were described in Chapter 3. Operationalising these
measures in the form of scales aimed at capturing
the actions required of those involved in initiating
and in implementing product innovation allowed
important differences to be identified between the
two groups of firms.
Taking the initiation of product innovation
first, it was found that innovative firms use
predominantly loose structures, whereas less
innovative firms use much more tightly structured
organisational arrangements. This is what one would
expect to find on the basis of previous research.
However, more specifically, in innovative firms
there is high role specialisation for initiating,
which is accompanied by medium functional
specialisation. Typically, in these firms the
marketing and engineering (R&D) functions are
intimately involved in idea generation, screening,

and concept development because these business
functions are most closely in touch with specialised
market needs. Less innovative firms, on the other
hand, exercise low levels of specialisation and
sometimes even leave the task for suggesting new
product ideas solely to the production function,
which is clearly less likely to produce ideas which
are both workable and marketable.

As has already been stated, the structural
properties in innovative firms are broadly as one
would expect during the phase of initiation.
Important exceptions are consistency in control
(a measure of standardisation) and centralisation.
This is because in the sample of active product
innovator firms ideas for new products are typically
encouraged for a specific market area delineated in
the firm's overall market plan. Only in one firm
were staff given what appeared to be complete
freedom to explore all new product ideas which might
catch their imagination.

Remarkably different structures were in evidence
for the purpose of implementing product innovation.
What is of particular interest here is that in both
groups of firms evidence was found of a shift in
structures between the initiation phase and the
implementation phase. However, as is explained
below, the shift in operating structures is
functional in the case of the active and experienced
product innovator firms but dysfunctional in firms
with less experience.

In the innovative firms high levels of
specialisation during implementation reflect the
involvement of a wide range of functions in product
development proper, test marketing and launching.
In these firms measurement of hidden structures
revealed a highly organised approach to tasks which
are closely watched over and controlled by top
management. Of particular importance is the use of
development manuals for ensuring that individual
projects are monitored against a standard set of
criteria. Overall, the methods of operation were
found to be quite different from those used for
initiating product innovation. This is in accord
with the analytical literature on innovation in
organisations, in which it is stressed that idea
generation and exploration require a certain freedom
of thought and action; whereas the implementation of
innovation requires a singleness of purpose.

What is of special interest is that the group of less innovative firms also experience a shift in their hidden structures between initiation and implementation. In their case, however, as has already been mentioned, the shift is dysfunctional for efficient product innovation. The reasons for this are not difficult to appreciate once the hidden structures for the two phases of initiation and implementation are examined. It has already been explained why the structures found in less innovative firms are dysfunctional for initiating new product ideas. What makes their structural arrangements unsuited for implementing is their very looseness. For example, only one less innovative firm was found to possess a development manual in which were spelled-out (in the form of check lists) tasks required of specific functions. But, in that particular firm it was not mandatory to adhere, even in spirit, to the procedures laid down in the manual! A particularly depressing feature, again identified by the working structures measured, was that while chief executive officers in this type of firm seek to retain tight control over development tasks, they manage to distance themselves from the consequences of new product development failures by ascribing responsibility for any failures to persons lower in the hierarchy.

A summary rating and a detailed analysis for each hidden structural measure for the phase of initiation (idea generation; screening; concept testing and development) and for the phase of implementation (product development proper; test marketing; launching) in the two groups of firms is given in Tables 4.2 and 4.3.

SUMMARY

This chapter provides the context for the investigations described in Chapters 5 and 6. The findings of the broader study described in the chapter show that there are very considerable differences in the way product innovation is organised in innovative as opposed to less innovative firms. Differences in both the formal and the hidden

The Context of the Cases

Table 4.2

ANALYSIS OF INITIATING STRUCTURES

Measure:	INNOVATIVE FIRMS N = 8		LESS INNOVATIVE FIRMS N = 8	
	Summary Rating	Scores	Summary Rating	Scores
SPECIALISATION				
i. Functional	MEDIUM	(-,8,-)*	LOW	(-,4,4)
ii. Role	HIGH	(6,2,-)	LOW	(-,3,5)
FORMALISATION				
i. Written guidance	LOW	(-,-,8)	LOW	(-,-,8)
ii. Written Communication	LOW	(-,-,8)	HIGH	(6,2,-)
STANDARDISATION				
i. Consistency in Control	MEDIUM	(1,5,2)	HIGH	(8,-,-)
ii. Frequency of reviews	LOW	(-,2,6)	LOW	(2,1,5)
CENTRALISATION Power retention by CEO	MEDIUM	(-,8,-)	HIGH	(7,1,-)
STRATIFICATION Seniority of dominant coalition	LOW	(-,2,6)	HIGH	(4,4,-)

* To be read: Of the 8 innovative firms (in terms of product innovation), none were scored high, 8 were scored medium, none low, in terms of functional specialisation. These scores resulted in a summary rating of MEDIUM.

Table 4.3

ANALYSIS OF IMPLEMENTING STRUCTURES

Measure:	INNOVATIVE FIRMS N = 8		LESS INNOVATIVE FIRMS N = 8	
	Summary Rating	Scores	Summary Rating	Scores
SPECIALISATION				
i. Functional	HIGH	(7,1,-)	LOW	(-,6,2)
ii. Role	HIGH	(6,2,-)	MEDIUM	(-,6,2)
FORMALISATION				
i. Written guidance	HIGH	(4,4,-)	LOW	(1,1,6)
ii. Written Communication	HIGH	(6,2,-)	MEDIUM	(2,4,2)
STANDARDISATION				
i. Consistency in Control	HIGH	(4,4,-)	LOW	(1,1,6)
ii. Frequency of reviews	HIGH	(5,2,1)	HIGH	(3,4,1)
CENTRALISATION				
Power retention by CEO	HIGH	(7,1,-)	HIGH	(4,4,-)
STRATIFICATION				
Seniority of dominant coalition	HIGH	(4,3,1)	MEDIUM	(2,5,1)

structures were identified in these firms. Analysis of the hidden structures provided particularly meaningful insights into why certain organisational arrangements are better suited for efficient product innovation. Loose structural arrangements were seen to be functional for initiation and tight structural arrangements functional for implementation in experienced product innovator firms. It was also shown that firms with less experience of the tasks involved display important differences in their informal structures which are less suited for efficient product innovation.

Chapter Five

HOW INNOVATIVE FIRMS ORGANISE

This chapter describes how three active and experienced product innovator firms organise for the purpose of speedily bringing new products to market. The methods used are described predominantly in the words of persons in these firms who are intimately involved in product innovation. The comments reported in the cases were elicited during the conduct of the wider study described in Chapter 4.

Each case illustrates a particular firm's approach to product innovation. The three cases have been selected because they illustrate three somewhat different approaches to speedy and efficient product innovation. Two of the firms are US-owned, the third is a smaller British-owned firm. As will become evident when reading the cases, the unifying theme is that in all the firms relatively loose initiating structures are followed by tight implementing structures. Confidences have been respected by disguising names and some of the material to safeguard proprietary know-how. Each case follows a standard pattern which allows ready comparison of all the cases.

HEWLETT-PACKARD : AN INSTRUMENT DIVISION

This division is one of the most innovative firms within the instrument industry. It is part of the US-owned Hewlett-Packard concern which is one of the world's most progressive companies in terms of management practices. The practices described in this chapter are of special interest because many have been adopted by other instrument manufacturing firms as a result of senior employees changing jobs within the industry.

BACKGROUND

The parent company of Hewlett-Packard (HP) was formed in 1939 by William Hewlett and David Packard. Although the company grew modestly during World War II and immediately thereafter, it was not until it broadened its test and measurement instrumentation product line in the 1950s that it began a period of sustained and substantial growth. In the late 1950s and early 1960s the company expanded operations in the US and established its first overseas subsidiaries in Europe, the UK, and in Japan. Also during this period, the company acquired a number of small, specialised firms in the medical and analytical fields. In the later 1960s HP greatly expanded the number of plant locations in the US and added plants in Brazil, Singapore and Malaysia. In 1966 the company entered the electronic data processing field with the introduction of its first computer. Limited conglomerate diversification began in the early 1970s with the acquisition of medical electronics and analytical instruments manufacturers.

Stopford et al (1980:500) have argued that the company continues to grow rapidly, based largely on new products developed in-house. Heavy R&D expenditure is used to develop new products, the cash revenue of which is healthy enough to expand capacity while the company remains virtually free of long-term debt. The company manufactures some of its integrated circuits and in 1981 employed 64,000 persons.

Hewlett-Packard is one of an increasing number of US firms which makes available an explicit list of corporate objectives to every employee. The list published in November 1980, in the form of a small booklet, highlights the following:

1. PROFIT OBJECTIVE: to achieve sufficient profit to finance company growth and to provide the resources needed to achieve other corporate objectives.

2. CUSTOMER OBJECTIVE: to provide products and services of the greatest possible value to customers, thereby gaining their respect and loyalty.

3. FIELDS OF INTEREST OBJECTIVE: to enter new fields only when the ideas together with technical, manufacturing and marketing skills assure that a needed and profitable contribution can be made.

4. GROWTH OBJECTIVE: to let growth be limited only by profits and the ability to develop and produce technical products that satisfy real customer needs.

5. OWN PEOPLE OBJECTIVE: to help HP people share in the company's success; to provide job security based on performance; to recognise individual achievements and to help them gain a sense of satisfaction and accomplishment from work.

6. MANAGEMENT OBJECTIVE: to foster initiative and creativity by allowing the individual great freedom of action in attaining well-defined objectives.

7. CITIZENSHIP OBJECTIVE: to honour obligations to society by being an economic, intellectual and social asset to each nation and each community in which HP operates.

The above corporate objectives are the base of HP's management philosophy. However, each part of the company is managed by a subsidiary set of objectives. For this purpose each employee is informed of "The HP way" in a booklet published under this title which has as its purpose to communicate the company's working philosophy or management style. The following excerpts have been selected as being representative of the messages intended to be communicated within this self-professed "people-orientated" company:

The Executive Vice President describes the total HP control structure in the corporate booklet as follows:

> The balance we strive for is to preserve the flexibility and freedom of action characteristic of a small company with marketing, technological and management strengths of a larger organization. The health of the organization lies within six product groups: Instruments, Computer Systems, Components, Medical, Calculators, Analytical.

> Each product group is characterised by having a common sales force for all of its divisions' products on a world-wide basis except for calculators which has two. The task is to match product offerings to the application needs of customers.

> Group managers set overall targets and continually review performance. They also set the strategic direction for the business they are in, and insure that the product programs of their divisions are complementary and make the important 'contribution' to the customer.

> The overall corporate organization has been designed to let the groups (with their divisions) concentrate on the product activities that they uniquely can do, without each having to understand and perform all the important administrative tasks of doing business on a world-wide basis.

The VP Corporate Services states:

> While the HP philosophy was quite visible

to us in those early years, management-by-
objective probably had its acid test in
1957, following the first management
meeting. At that meeting it was decided
to reorganize the company along more
structured lines, with Bill (Hewlett) and
Dave (Packard) delegating the functional
responsibilities they had held. The R&D
activity was set up into four lab groups.
I'll never forget the sight of Packard
walking past the microwave lab, not saying
a thing. It must have been hard for them
to pull out that way, but they stuck to it
. . . To me, that management meeting and
the changes that occurred as a result of
it were a landmark for the company. I
think it proved that we could change and
that we could not only preserve our
management philosophy but also strengthen
it. Growth could happen without our
having to give up the good things that
make HP different. A lot of companies
never make it past that point - remaining
small or changing their style - because
top management didn't know how to let go.

The VP of the Instruments Group states:

The art of getting things done through
people is fairly simple when operations
are small. As we become more complex
organizations, with interactive product
lines and international markets, the art
is to simplify lines of authority. We
need to give people a clear sense of
objectives and a clearly defined
responsibility they can understand. To
bring this off, we are going to have to
develop a new breed of managers who will
be able to manage on a multi-plant, multinational, multi-product basis, yet provide
all the traditional strengths of a local
manager.

The Innovative Firms

The VP of the Computer Systems Group states:

> The starting point for management by
> objectives in a division should be an
> overall set of short and long range
> objectives that have the acceptance and
> support of group and corporate management.
> These division objectives serve as the
> framework for all further decision making
> and planning, and therefore should be
> broadly visible. Each functional manager
> (R&D, Marketing, Product Assurance,
> Personnel, Manufacturing and Finance) is
> responsible for ensuring that these
> overall objectives are understood by all
> members of the team. More importantly,
> each manager is expected to secure the
> team's commitment in spirit to the
> objectives. Within the framework the
> functional managers then establish
> objectives for their areas. As before,
> each functional manager consults with the
> team in establishing them and reviews them
> with the general manager to ensure they
> mesh with the division and other
> functional area objectives. This process
> is repeated at each level until all
> managers have developed objectives to
> guide their team, each team member is
> committed to the objectives, and all plans
> mesh both horizontally and vertically.

The VP Personnel states:

> Once a division or a department has
> developed a tactical plan of its own - a
> set of working objectives that are in
> essential agreement with corporate
> objectives - it's important for managers
> and supervisors to keep in good operating
> condition. This is where observation,
> measurement, feedback and guidance come
> in. It's what I call 'management by
> wandering around'. Management by
> wandering around is how you find out
> whether you're on track and heading at the

right speed in the right direction. If you don't constantly monitor how people are operating, not only will they tend to wander off track but also they will begin to believe you weren't serious about the plan in the first place . . . by wandering around I literally mean moving around and talking to people . . . you start out by being accessible and approachable, but the main thing is to realize that you're here to listen. The second is that it is vital to keep people informed about what's going on in the company, especially those things which are important to them. The third reason for doing this is because it is just plain fun.

The General Manager, Avondale Division states:

Divisions are normally organized into six functional areas: R&D, manufacturing, marketing, finance, product assurance and personnel. The first three are typically called line functions. This means that they have the primary responsibility for the overall success of the product line. Finance, product assurance and personnel are normally thought of as staff functions which provide important information and assistance to the line functions to help them carry out their responsibilities more effectively . . . It is important to remember that, while the autonomy of a division is one of HP's strengths, it is our ability to work together and to transfer technology and ideas across divisional lines that has really made HP so strong.

The US Eastern Sales Region's Instrument Manager states:

In the face of a steady growth in corporate size and complexity, a contin-

uing challenge for Hewlett-Packard has
been to ensure the most direct possible
link between its product organization and
the needs of its customers. Certainly,
the sales organization is somewhat complex
when viewed on paper: teams of field
engineers locally supported by regional
and country organizations, sharing common
offices, services and policies, and all
requiring the attention of more than 30
factory organizations. How does the HP
way operate in this setting?

There is first the organizational answer:
field teams and the factory divisions are
organized into six product related groups
which provide the necessary cohesion and
identity. But the main answer is still
the HP principle of getting the job done
at the most fundamental levels of the
organization. For the greatest part of
their activities, the field engineers will
be in direct contact with the divisional
sales engineers. When problems or special
circumstances come up, the district
manager will be in touch with the divisional sales manager - and so on. They
have a direct working relationship with
the people who can give them answers.

We now turn to consider the specific operations of
an Instrument Division of Hewlett-Packard. The
Division's Marketing Manager commented on the
current management style in the following words:

All employees in HP enjoy the same nominal
status. All are paid monthly. All eat in
the same canteen normally. All employees
are given very detailed information on
company performance. All are encouraged
to participate in stock purchase schemes
and so are informed daily about HP share
price levels. All employees wear name
badges in what are usually open plan
offices. In the divisions the GM
typically sits in the centre of a well-
laid out manufacturing, R&D, marketing,

finance, etc. activity. He is visible to all.

HP is a rather unique company. It has a rather unique set of personnel policies which are seen as progressive in the US, particularly as far as keeping a small company atmosphere is concerned, with for example, first names always being used. The company has a policy of no redundancy. If the company runs into a shortage of orders, we run a shorter week and we all accept say 80% of our salary for a four day week. This has not, as yet, happened in my own division but it has happened in certain other divisions. Rarely is someone asked to leave for disciplinary reasons. 1000 employees is seen as the ideal size for a division - 2000 would be the maximum.

THE FORMAL STRUCTURE

There is a formally issued organisation chart at the Instrument Division, but it is frequently out of date. The division is headed by a General Manager who sits literally in the centre of activity at the manufacturing plant in one large open plan office/factory/despatch area. The current allocation of responsibilities is shown in Table 5.1.

It can be seen that the organisation is structured to deal formally not only with the tasks of managing the existing product range, but also with the task of investigating and developing new products. In fact, marketing and R&D personnel in most HP divisions typically spend as much time and money on exploring and exploiting new products as they do on managing existing products. After all, innovative firms rely on fast returns from the market from R&D-based new product ventures, whilst less innovative firms tend to concentrate their efforts in wringing the last bit of operating profit from older products.

It is especially important to note that this firm has not appointed new product managers. The task of handling new products is the responsibility of the Product Marketing Managers, and below them of the Product Managers, both working very closely with their technical counterparts, as is shown in Table 5.1. Whilst the establishment of New Product Managers (or Product Planners as they are called in some firms) has been considered from time to time such an alternative organisational arrangement has been rejected so far in the Division because it is felt that all personnel should place equal importance on managing existing products as they do on managing new products.

Table 5.1

HP INSTRUMENT DIVISION - EXECUTIVE CONTROL STRUCTURE

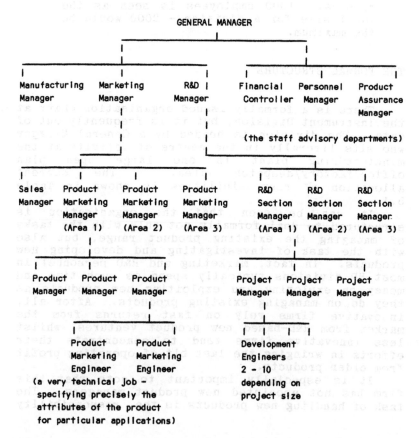

THE HIDDEN STRUCTURES

For initiating product innovation

Asked where ideas for possible new products come from the Marketing Manager commented:

> To answer this we need to differentiate between possible new products for (1) markets in which we have experience and, (2) markets which we do not know well. In the case of the markets we know, successful product development is crucial to maintain market position. Any short-comings here are readily observable. The task of product innovation in markets known to us is delegated to the relevant Product Marketing Manager and the relevant R&D Section Manager. I suppose you could call all this 'related product innovation'.
>
> Turning now to possible new products for markets not at present well-known to us, the fundamental question is where to get the ideas. That can be from many sources - it can be from outside the company; it can be suggested from on-going development work in markets known to us, but the important point is that it requires someone in our Division to connect related product innovation with the needs of potential new markets. We cannot expect our existing customers to do this for us. We have found that when we ask our existing customers what new products they want, they will almost always ask for more of known capabilities. However, we see our task here as putting together several capabilities for our customers, in a way they have not thought of. In this sense our radically new products are, I suppose, really a combination of say 4, 5 or 6 new products. That's why it takes us a relatively long time to develop them - especially because many of our new products now have integrated computer control. All this requires working very closely with our customers, but it's us

who normally do all the putting together
for their benefit - that's the unique
service we offer prior to making available
a new product which it is extremely
difficult for one of our competitors to
copy. I suppose in this sense we are
seeking to provide our customers with a
system of technologically related
products, rather than just a single new
product. Interestingly, we often get our
inspiration for a new system from another
customer base.

I mentioned earlier that ideas for
'unrelated product development' can come
from outside the company. Sometimes
bright development engineers approach us
with possible new product ideas, saying
that the potential new product would
broaden our range. We get a lot of such
suggestions - people write in with their
ideas saying they want to work with us in
developing them. Often the ideas are very
good, but we have to reject them because
the market is too small; or, commonly, the
product is not suited to the talents of
our existing sales force. Our own HP labs
come up with similar new technical ideas
for possible new products. We then have
to decide whether we can use them. I suppose we could call the first type of ideas
"spurious extraneous technical inputs';
the latter 'internal technology push'.

We rarely have brainstorming sessions,
because as you can see, we get a constant
flow of ideas for possible new products.
This really puts the emphasis on evaluating the ideas. It really is not too
difficult to come up with ideas, and as I
have said we get plenty suggested to us,
but the most difficult problem is apprai-
sing whether the idea is likely to lead to
a new product which fits in with divisional objectives. Don't forget ideas for
possible new products are being constantly
bounced around verbally - it is true to
say that the General Manager is continually being bombarded with such ideas -
the trick is to pick the right ideas.

Essentially, I suppose we are in the business of speculative new product development. We do not take on development contracts - that would make us dependent on others, but we do take on some supply contracts. However, whenever we develop a new product we do so for a world market which we consider is worth addressing.

Although our systems for monitoring work here are reasonably formal in so far as assessing progress is concerned, meetings on possible new projects are essentially informal. If a plausible project idea begins to harden out the relevant Product Marketing Manager and R&D Section Manager will begin to involve themselves and will agree that an evaluation study should be done. . . . it's all very informal . . . It's a decision to study a project . . . Not a lot of money will be spent - probably around $20,000 for trips to talk to potential customers at home and overseas, as well as about two months' work for the two managers. They are often collecting the necessary information as part of their other duties - they may be working on two or three new potential projects at any one time.

Essentially, however, remember that we see by far the most of our new products coming from the market areas which we are already active in. It is because of this that we rely almost exclusively on our Product Marketing Managers and our R&D Section Managers for product innovation. It is crucial to remember that we are working in an area where it is not possible to have good bright ideas unless you are really on top of the relevant technology. It is because of this that we find the best ideas for new products come from market areas in which we are already active. All the time, however, it is market areas and their changing demands we are focusing on. If this means changing our product offering, then that's the business we are in.

It would be true to say that our major
thrust as far as developing new products
is concerned, as I have said, is with
developing products for markets known to
us. Our division is not really in the
speculative new venture business. Certain
parts of HP are, but we are really
providing an instrument service for known
types of markets.

For evaluating alternatives

Commenting on evaluation procedures the
Marketing Manager stated:

We are constantly looking to see whether
there is synergy between possible new
products and our corporate and divisional
resources. The decision on whether or not
to go into product market areas which are
unrelated to our present operations is
taken by the General Manager in
conjunction with the Marketing and R&D
Manager. This means that ideas for
unrelated product/market innovation go
through a finer screening mesh than do
ideas for possible related new products.

We are very conscious of the need to
constantly worry about the sort of market
areas we are addressing. I personally
believe that many companies in the high
technology field unconsciously spread
themselves too widely in unrelated
markets. This does not allow them to
offer a specialised service to selected
markets. I suppose in this sense our
methods for product innovation are highly
disciplined - we know we have the
development capability, but the most
important task is to ensure that we will
make money and grow with the help of the
new product. All the time, remember that
we have a responsibility not only to our
own Division but also to the other parts
of HP. Sometimes we will come up with
ideas for possible new products which are
better suited to another division - and we
will pass these across.

Typically, as I have said, a new product
will result from an investigation carried
out by a Product Marketing Manager and a
R&D Section Manager. If the project is
approved, it is passed on to a product
manager and a project manager to handle in
concert. Before approval each project
will have gone through a project
evaluating meeting at which all heads of
departments (including the staff
departments) are present. The project
will be presented by the relevant Product
Marketing Manager and the relevant R&D
Section Manager formally at this meeting.
It will be checked against a certain
number of screening factors which are
closely related to the Division's
objectives.

Project evaluation meetings are held when
there are projects to be evaluated. Yes,
we do formally sit around a table
together, but that's it. One of the
advantages of a firm like ours is that
there are always more good projects which
could be undertaken than there are
resources available to undertake them. So
the skill comes in selecting the projects
with the best potential. One important
question which is always asked is 'Does
the project lead us somewhere we want to
be in the future? . . . But now we are
turning to strategic issues and for this
purpose we do have formal and regular
meetings annually to check that we are
heading in the direction we want to head
as a Division. Usually all the senior
members of the marketing and R&D
departments will go away for 2 days to a
hotel to do this. There the focus is on
new projects and whether they will lead us
into market areas where there is a future
for us. Included in this review are
projects currently under development - all
are ranked according to their usefulness
to us. You see, we will have a certain
number of projects under development at
any one time and there will be an ample
number in the queue waiting to be

developed, perhaps to replace a project which has been stopped. Essentially it's an annual product planning meeting.

For implementing product innovation

The Engineering Manager stated:

Once a project has been given the formal go ahead at the initial evaluation meeting attended by all the main managers of the Division, it becomes the direct joint responsibility of a product manager and a R&D project manager. Their direct bosses, the Product Marketing Manager and the R&D Section Manager will, of course, be watching progress - indeed, they will be watching progress on several projects and they will also be considering potential new projects to put forward. It is, after all, their responsibility to see that profits are increasingly being generated from their market area.

It typically takes from 3 to 4 years to develop a new project into a marketable product. If it becomes obvious that there is no real future, the project is cancelled. Of course, ideally, it should cost less to finish a project which has been under development for say 2 or 3 years than it will cost to start a new one. But it's the ultimate return from the market place which interests us.

A R&D Project Manager commented:

Project managers are expected to informally monitor their projects daily. For this purpose they can use any method - usually a bar chart is used. Formal evaluation takes place at 5 separate formal checkpoints for which we have specially designed pro-forma documentation. Again we are given discretion over how the information is presented to those attending checkpoint meetings. You can see from the sheets that every project has to be signed off at each of the 5 stages by each of the participating managers.

70

Whilst R&D project managers are given considerable freedom in how they pursue particular ventures, the General Manager does keep in detailed touch with developments. In fact, he can tell you at any one point of time the exact stage of development of each project. He is constantly walking into the development laboratory to ask questions about progress.

Typically it takes some 5 years to develop a radically new product. Working backwards it takes us a year to get from the final product design to actual manufacture, because the testing requirements are so extensive before launch. Initiation, i.e. from idea to project appraisal takes typically a year, meaning that the actual project development time is on average some 2 or 3 years. These are extended periods of time, but don't forget that our products are very complex - they are rather like 4 or 5 separate new products combined for specific market applications. We are, after all, in the top end of the instrument market. The periods between the checkpoints really represent a fairly smooth flow of activities - you see, we are in the business of developing rather advanced new products, and we are therefore prepared to approach the task in a disciplined way.

SCORING OF THE HIDDEN STRUCTURES

On the basis of interview data collected within this division of HP (relevant excerpts of which have been reported above verbatim), the firm's working structures were scored as shown in Tables 5.2 and 5.3.

The Innovative Firms

Table 5.2

HP STRUCTURES FOR INITIATING PRODUCT INNOVATION

1.1 Specialisation

(i) Do ideas for possible new products stem predominantly from one department, or do several departments involve themselves intimately in this task? (Functional specialisation)

Low	☐	One function only
	☒	Marketing and R&D
High	☐	Marketing, R&D and other(s)

(ii) By what means do those suggesting ideas get their inspiration? Are any specific activities engaged in – like brainstorming sessions – to increase the potential number of ideas? (Role specialisation)

Low	☐	Ad hoc
	☐	Ad hoc and analytical techniques e.g. lost orders, exhibitions, market surveys
High	☒	Ad hoc and analytical techniques, and regular and formal brainstorming, buzz sessions etc

1.2 Formalisation

(i) To what extent are those who involve themselves in suggesting ideas for possible new products given guidance or guidelines on this task in writing? (Written guidance)

Low	☒	Not at all
	☐	To some extent
High	☐	Extensively

(ii) To what extent is information on ideas for possible new products exchanged in writing between those involved? (Written communication)

Low	☒	Predominantly spoken
	☐	More spoken than written
High	☐	More written than spoken

HP STRUCTURES FOR INITIATING PRODUCT INNOVATION continued

1.3 Standardisation

(i)   What guidance is given on the sort of new product ideas the company is seeking? (Consistency in control)

    Low   ☒ Business mission delineated

              ☐ Product market area delineated

    High   ☐ Product area delineated

(ii) How frequently are formal meetings held at which suggestions for possible new products are discussed? (Frequency of reviews)

    Low   ☐ Less frequently than every 3 months

              ☒ At between 1 month and 3 monthly intervals

    High   ☐ Monthly or more frequently

1.4 Centralisation

How much influence does the CEO exert over the flow of ideas for possible new products? (Power retention by CEO)

    Low   ☐ He encourages as many ideas to be put forward as possible - the more the merrier

              ☒ He encourages ideas within the confines of the delineated strategy

    High   ☐ He seeks to keep tight control over the sort of ideas which are put forward

1.5 Stratification

From what level in the organisation are ideas typically taken up? (Seniority of dominant coalition)

    Low   ☒ Departmental executive level

              ☐ H O D level

    High   ☐ Board level

73

The Innovative Firms

Table 5.3

<u>HP STRUCTURES FOR IMPLEMENTING PRODUCT INNOVATION</u>

2.1   <u>Specialisation</u>

(I)   Which department or departments are intimately involved in the development process? (Functional specialisation)

       Low   ☐   R&D

                   ☐   Marketing and R&D

       High   ☒   Marketing, R&D and other(s)

(II)   Certain types of activities can be particularly important in the development process. Do you, for example, have persons who assume responsibility for the following roles? (Role specialisation)

(1)   Business/project management (i.e. product championship)
(2)   Entrepreneurial interpretation of market trends (market gatekeeping)
(3)   Analysis of scientific and engineering trends affecting the development (technical gatekeeping)
(4)   Manufacturing/quality gatekeeping
(5)   Godfathering (sponsorship by a senior member)

       Low   ☐   2 or less roles are specifically provided for

                   ☐   3-4 roles are specifically provided for

       High   ☒   All roles are specifically provided for

2.2   <u>Formalisation</u>

(I)   In what form are those involved in the development process given guidance or guidelines on their work? (Written guidance)

       Low   ☐   The process is explained verbally

                   ☐   Some written guidelines are given

       High   ☒   A control manual is provided

(II)   In what way is progress on specific development tasks noted? (Written communication)

       Low   ☐   Informal notes are kept

                   ☐   Formal notes are issued as required

       High   ☒   Formal minutes of meetings are issued

74

HP STRUCTURES FOR IMPLEMENTING PRODUCT INNOVATION continued

2.3   Standardisation

(i)   Are the same development criteria applied to control each project? For example, has each project an equal chance of being stopped? (Consistency in control)

      Low   ☐ Totally different criteria

                  ☐ Somewhat different criteria

      High   ☒ Essentially similar criteria

(ii)   How frequently is progress on development work monitored formally? (Frequency of reviews)

      Low   ☐ Less frequently than every 3 months

                  ☐ At between 1 month and 3 monthly intervals

      High   ☒ Monthly or more frequently

2.4   Centralisation

What control or influence does the CEO exert over the development work? (Power retention by CEO)

      Low   ☐ He expects others to get on with it independently

                  ☐ He is kept in touch with progress

      High   ☒ He is informed of progress in detail

2.5   Stratification

At what level is responsibility for the overall success of a project development assumed i.e. at whom is the finger pointed if something goes wrong? (Seniority of dominant coalition)

      Low   ☐ Department executive level

                  ☐ H O D level

      High   ☒ Board level

The Innovative Firms

SUMMARY

We see how in this firm product innovation is an accepted way of life. This is evidenced, in part, by the fact that separate new product managers have not been appointed to work in parallel with the marketing and technical managers for existing products. Everyone in this firm has been made aware that a high technology firm must rely on effective product innovation to remain competitive.

Because the firm is peopled by lively members of staff, there is no shortage of ideas for possible new products to choose from. There can be little doubt that the predominantly loose informal or hidden structure contributes to this phenonemon. However, what emerges as striking is the care with which new products are evaluated. Typically we see these being filtered at quite a high level (by Product Marketing and R&D Section Managers) who are responsible for the performance of their business area.

To recapitulate: the initiation procedures comprise two main phases. First, a new product idea is proposed by or to the relevant Product Marketing and R&D Section Manager, who between them are effectively responsible for initial screening against divisional objectives. Second, as a result of an investigation costing typically some $20,000, a firmer definition is determined for the possible new product. The purpose of this initial investigation is to see whether a new product could be developed which will make money in the intended business area. This work is approved and overseen jointly by a Product Marketing and R&D Section Manager. At the successful conclusion of an initial investigation the idea for a new product is considered at a Definition Release Meeting at which money is hopefully released for its further development.

After successful release at the definition stage, an abrupt change in operating procedures is in evidence. Whereas during initiation those involved were given considerable freedom to explore alternative courses of action, the period of implementation is marked by a formal series of checkpoints at which progress is monitored against a standard set of criteria. The key implementation phases are listed below:

1. Design phase leading to a satisfactory laboratory prototype. Progress is checked at a formal <u>Design Release Meeting</u>.

2. Prototype units are produced, normally 5-7. Assembly and test procedures are laid down. A manufacturing specification is agreed. Manuals are prepared for servicing and operation. Progress is checked at a formal <u>Manufacturing Release Meeting</u>.

3. Line assembly procedures are agreed, Test procedures are agreed. The product specification is reviewed against the Division's objectives. Quality assurance standards are checked again. Agreement is reached between all functions. Progress is checked at a formal <u>Divisional Manager Release Meeting</u>.

4. Everyone involved signs that the tasks required for successful formal shipment have been completed and that continuous testing has been completed. Progress is checked at the formal <u>Shipment Release Meeting</u>.

5. A last check is performed on the feasibility of production, responsibility for which is now transferred formally to manufacturing. Progress is checked at the formal <u>R&D Release Meeting</u>.

JOHN FLUKE MANUFACTURING COMPANY INC.

This company is at an extremely interesting stage of development become its formal organisation structure remains predominantly centralised. As will be seen, however, the informal or hidden structures adopted are extremely well-suited for efficient product innovation. Whilst Fluke has not grown to the size of HP as a whole, it has done extremely well in terms of corporate development and the satisfaction it provides to its employees.

BACKGROUND

Fluke is among the largest firms in test and measurement instrument manufacturing with a broad product line. Established in 1948 in the basement of Mr & Mrs John Fluke's home in Connecticut the company now employs over 3000 people and recently moved into a prestigious new headquarters in Seattle, Washington. It was in 1952 that the company moved to Seattle (home of the Boeing Corporation). In its early years the company acquired technology from outside sources - in 1963 Montronics Inc. a small Montana firm with frequency synthesizer capability was bought. In 1973 another acquisition, Trendar Corporation in Mountain View, California put Fluke into the ATE market with digital board testers. Since that time all new products have come from inside the company and normally all development work is funded internally. Outside funds have, however, been used to finance plant and some capital items.

The company's business is designing, producing and selling electronic test and measuring equipment. It markets over 100 discrete product lines, each of which typically has several options. The company is organised on a truly marketing-orientated basis - the 1981 Annual Report analysed strengths and weaknesses in specific markets as shown in Table 5.4. The Report justifies activities over such a wide product range as providing a cushion against the effects of economic cycles in three main market application areas:

1   General test and service applications
2   Precision measurement applications
3   Automated control applications

The Report states that it is these market areas which have provided the rationale for establishing the three company divisions detailed in Table 5.5

TABLE 5.4

FLUKE STRENGTHS IN IDENTIFIED PRODUCT MARKETS

MARKETS (PRODUCT TYPES)	DMMs	Calibrators	Signal sources	Counters	Board testers	Measurement insts.	Data loggers	IEEE bus controllers	Micro-system testers
Electronics: R&D	1	1	1	0	3	0	3	1	1
Electronics: Production	1	1	1	0	3	0	3	1	1
Electronics: Service	1	1	1	0	3	0	3	1	1
Electronics: Metrology	1	1	1	0	3	-	3	1	-
Electronics: OEM	1	1	1	0	3	0	3	1	1
Defence, Government	1	1	1	0	3	0	3	1	1
Industrial	1	1	1	0	3	0	3	1	1
Distribution	1	1	-	-	3	-	3	-	-
Consumer	1	1	-	0	3	-	3	-	-
Communication	1	1	1	0	3	0	3	1	1

1 = Leader in market
3 = 2nd or 3rd in market
0 = Some market presence

Source: Fluke 1981 Annual Report

THE FORMAL STRUCTURE

The company divisionalised its operations in the Autumn of 1980 when Business Units were formally assigned to one of three separate Divisions, as is shown in Table 5.5. Mr John Fluke, the founder, still exerts a dominating influence on company activities, but it is expected that he will delegate certain responsibilities soon (he is in his early 70s). Mr Fluke is at his desk at 7.00 a.m. every morning. All executives report direct to the COO - Mr Zevenbergen - who is Mr Fluke's right-hand man, meaning that control structure is extremely tight at the top.

A Vice-President commented on the formal organisation structure as follows:

> We seek to decentralise our company operations through Business Units, of which there are several in each of the three operating divisions. The aim has been to promote the entrepreneural spirit within BUs. So, rather than grand directives coming down from the top concerning the product markets we should be in, we have tended to say 'We are giving you in the Business Units a lot of opportunities and flexibility. We want you to identify new business opportunities and when you feel strongly enough we want you to speak up and ask for money to pursue particular avenues'.

> You see, from the outside, we look like a broad-line instrument company - that's good. From the inside, however, we don't feel that way - we feel that we are successful in some major product areas and that we have yet to prove ourselves in some of the others. Internally, we are not totally happy with our diversification efforts, because we would not regard ourselves as a success until we are No.1 in a particular market.

> We have established our Business Units around markets and products. We are particularly interested in identifying clusters of customers where the number of customers involved is of manageable proportions -

Table 5.5

FLUKE EXECUTIVE CONTROL STRUCTURE

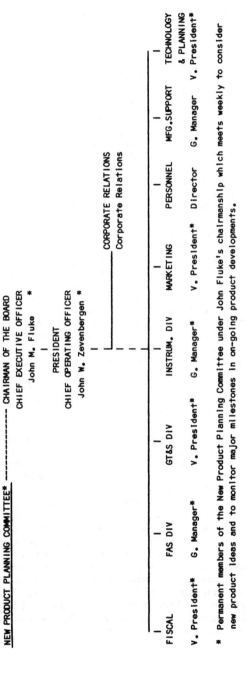

* Permanent members of the New Product Planning Committee under John Fluke's chairmanship which meets weekly to consider new product ideas and to monitor major milestones in on-going product developments.

such as for example calibration customers, of whom there are several thousand, all of whom we are in touch with. There are other markets, however, as in the case of our voltmeters, where the range of customers is extremely diverse and numerous, where the Business Unit's major focus is on the type of product being produced. All the time, though, we are watching to see whether there are special opportunities within the broad range of customers. Once these are identified, it might well lead to intercompany conflicts, because the products of a particular BU destined for a particular market segment might have to be supplemented by products from another BU. This causes us problems with transfer prices, service requirements and stocking policies. These are the growing pains of a successful business. Yes, we envisage that successful BUs might ultimately evolve into semi-autonomous operating units, as is the case with HP divisions. We still group our BUs into divisions, primarily on the basis of management expediency, rather than in accordance with the General Electric schema of company sector strengths. All this is gradually evolving in the company - we don't have any magic answers, but we do know that we need to keep in close touch with market developments in those sectors where we are keen to compete.

You see, in the past we have built a lot of general purpose products which had appeal to a very wide customer base. We never really worried about the exact way in which they were being used, apart from establishing some broad generalities about the type of testing being undertaken. However, we see applications beginning to cluster now, and we see success going to instrument companies in the future which are best at interpreting their customer's precise demands and which then market a product which really meets a specific type of demand. You see, a company like ours has the ability to make a tremendous range of sophisticated products.

We need to develop products, however, which
meet technical applications with a market
future.

Our company is at a particularly
interesting stage of development. We are
market orientated and we accept the need to
finance appropriate strategies in relation
to identified market segments. It will be
interesting to see what our dominant
orientation will be in the future - will it
be employee-centred, as in the case of HP,
or engineering-centred as in the case of
Tektronix?

Yes, in one sense we have a tremendous
amount of control from the top as far as
product innovation is concerned, yet in
another we have almost no control. We have
made no attempt to tie the short-term
product innovation budgets of individual
Business Units to the overall company
planning process. Every quarter we have
strategy meetings with all the Business
Units - to see where we are spending
development monies. These strategy
meetings allow the top officers to comment
on the overall direction of product
development within the company. So,
really, we take a very broad look from the
top at the type of products being planned
to ensure they fit in with corporate plans.
But we look for the initiative for the
actual type of product innovation at the
Business Unit level. Normally, initiatives
will be channelled to the Manager of the
Business Unit, who will release funds for
the development. In the past, individuals
used to go straight to John Fluke for
money, but as we have grown in size the
system has become more formal.

Business Unit Marketing Manager:

Business Units have been given
responsibilities for both current
operations as well as product innovation.
My Business Unit deals with a specific end-
user industry. Specifically, we serve the
market made up of firms servicing certain

microprocessor controlled products. I have
product managers reporting to me who
provide sales support for our established
product lines. I am also responsible for
new product development, which we do in
conjunction with the engineering function.
We attach equal importance to running our
existing product lines as we do to
developing new products. This is shown by
product planning managers and product
managers being on the same level of pay.

We are very anxious to ensure that product
planners have an orientation which is
somewhat different from that of the product
specialists. The 9000 series would almost
certainly not have been developed had
development been left to the existing
product managers – they would have
encouraged the development of a better
oscilloscope, because that was the product
they were familiar with, rather than a
logic analyser. Of course we want follow-
ons to existing lines, but we also want
people whose responsibility it is to look
at the wider market requirements and
particularly at how these are changing.

Business Unit Engineering Manager:

We employ Product Planning Managers and
specialists who have a development
engineering background and also a training
in marketing. Their job is to do market
research, particularly how a market might
be segmented. Once they have identified a
worthwhile and accessible segment their job
is to dream up a suitable product
specification. I must emphasise that
marketing within a Business Unit is
primarily product planning and sales
support, because selling is done centrally.
[The way marketing is organised within
Business Units is shown in Table 5.6.] A
product planner will work very closely
indeed with engineering – he will
communicate at any level with engineering
people – we are not hierarchically
structured. If the new
product he has dreamt up is developed

successfully by engineering, he may well be appointed to act as its product manager ultimately. Typically, product planners are people who want to supplement their technical experience with marketing action.

Product planners are not the only people dreaming up new products for particular market segments - often they do it in conjunction with a project engineer 'without portfolio', i.e. one who is not formally involved in a particular product development project.

Table 5.6

FLUKE TYPICAL BUSINESS UNIT ORGANISATION

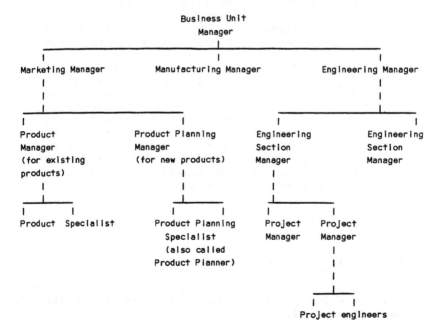

Business Unit Marketing Manager:

> If you reflect on how Business Units are
> established, you will see that each
> addresses identified segments of demand.
> Usually, because the segments are growing,
> the Business Unit Manager does not have as
> many products as he would like - hence the
> product planner has many market
> opportunities to consider. It is the
> product planner who will write the
> expenditure proposal which the Business
> Unit Manager will use in justifying his
> engineering expenditure to top management.
> Usually the product proposal will be
> written in conjunction with a project
> engineer, but in the first instance it is
> up to the product planner to sell the ideas
> to the Business Unit Manager.

> When a product manager is exploring
> possibilities for selling existing products
> into completely new markets, which a
> product planner may also be exploring for
> the purpose of selling new products, then
> they have to work together, and that is
> when my advice will be sought. The system
> of product managers and product planning
> managers is not religiously adhered to
> throughout the company. In some Business
> Units, where the products are more mature,
> we have product planners who report direct
> to a product manager - that's because we
> want to watch that the new product lines do
> not conflict dysfunctionally with existing
> product lines in known markets.

THE HIDDEN STRUCTURES

For initiating product innovation

Asked at what level in a Business Unit really
new ideas for product innovation occur the Marketing
Manager replied:

> Typically, product innovation will be
> initiated by a Product Planning Manager in

86

conjunction with an Engineering Section Manager to define a high technology product for a new market. That is exactly how my Business Unit got started. The team built up later to a task force which when in full-swing included over 10 people from marketing, engineering and manufacturing.

Business Unit Engineering Manager:

We do occasionally have brain-storming sessions to make sure we have not overlooked a new opportunity. We use it as a mechanism to widen our vision of the market. However, there is always a temptation in a successful manufacturing company to think that you know it all and that you understand the market place perhaps even better than your customers. In this way you become arrogant in your design of new products as you spring these on your customers. Because of this we now tend to build prototypes of new products and to check these out with certain selected customers. This is important on two counts: (1) externally, so that we can see the reaction of potential customers, and (2) internally, so that we can explain the new product's performance features to our own management, because often the new product will be based on a technology which is different from the one which has traditionally been offered to the customer.

It was particularly true in the case of the 9000, where we set out to design a more sophisticated storage oscilloscope, but ended up with a revolutionary logic analyser. I can tell you in the case of that product there were some disappointed people around whose hearts were set on developing a better 'scope'.

I think it is extremely important to acknowledge that as suppliers we do not have an inalienable right to specify our customer's next variant of product. Going out to show a prototype to selected customers has now become the accepted practice here, and it represents a major change in the way we initiate product innovation. Previously we were excessively secretive - we were too product-orientated. Now we listen far more carefully to what our potential customers are saying, and out of these comments design a new product.

Business Unit Manager:

The big advantage in showing customers a mock-up of the new product is that they can then suggest additional features which could be incorporated. In the case of the 9000 we got a lot of useful information that way. This was all before a formal expenditure proposal was put to top management for the required capital expenditure. So you see, we did a lot of spadework before committing ourselves to a proposal.

I want to emphasise that sometimes a Product Planning Manager will put forward an outline proposal of 2 or 3 sides to the New Product Planning Committee, even when the Manager doesn't have a ghost of an idea what the new product might look like. If the Committee likes the idea it will release quite large amounts of money to undertake preliminary market research aimed at quantifying the likely potential for the new product. Sometimes monies are even released for this purpose by the Committee to fortunate bright young engineers.

At this preliminary stage we are very loosely structured and so meetings are organised as and when they are required. Nothing really gets very formal until the time when a full-blown proposal is put to the New Product Planning Committee for the release of a lot of money. I do want to emphasise that we attach great importance in doing a lot of spadework before asking the Committee to grant us funds for a full-scale programme of development. After all, this is essential if you want to be pretty sure of success - both for yourself as an individual, and for the company as a provider of the funds.

For evaluating alternatives

Outline proposals requesting approval for preliminary market research expenditures are typically put to the New Product Planning Committee by a Business Unit Manager on behalf of a Product Planning Manager and an Engineering Section Manager. If after having spent quite large amounts of money it still looks as though the new product idea is viable, a further request is made by the Business Unit Manager to be allowed to submit a formal expenditure proposal. Before the formal expenditure proposal is tabled further funds might need to be released by the New Product Planning Committee to cover the cost of formal market research on which profit projections will be based. The formal expenditure proposal is then submitted in a strictly standard way by the Business Unit Manager to the New Product Planning Committee for consideration at one of its weekly meetings. (For the composition of the Committee see Table 5.5).

For implementing product innovation

The procedures for implementing were commented on by a Project Engineer as follows:

One important result of having to submit formal expenditure proposals to the New Product Planning Committee in a standard way is that we get prepared to follow a standard operating procedure for developing the product once it is approved. Yes, we certainly do follow the procedures laid down in the thick Product Development Manual, but not over-religiously. After all, there are things in there which are more appropriate to the development of analogue instruments rather than to new digital instruments.

Specific check-lists are contained in the Manual for all implementation activities, all of which have to be checked by or agreed with the following functions:

1. Marketing   4. Finance
2. Engineering   5. Quality Assurance
3. Manufacturing 6. Product Safety

The phases are as follows:

1. Prototype development, leading to Prototype Release.

2. Design development, leading to Design Release.

3. Hardmodel development, leading to Hardmodel Release.

4. First batch production, leading to Manufacturing Release.

5. Full production, leading to Production Release.

As is stated in our standard operating instructions a formal expenditure proposal is regarded very much as a living document, which is updated as we go along. Actual development progress is tracked at weekly progress meetings within the Business Units - it used to be done by the New Product Planning Committee, but only the major release points (see above) are checked centrally now.

Yes, sir, product developments are stopped - I can think of a number of recent examples - the 820 and the 1150 - it happens when the evaluation criteria are not met and it becomes evident that they will never be met. When this happens there are no hard feelings - it's just that there are better things to spend our money on.

BU Engineering Manager:

Yes, the formal release points are taken very seriously. It is true that sometimes we bend the rules, but that is done quite deliberately. As a normal rule all main aspects are checked, as prescribed in the Product Development Manual.

Every project has a manager - it being his responsibility to see that it is brought off as far as development work is concerned. This is usually the product planner, who can expect to become the product manager for the new product and so he sets about planning its introduction to the market. This is typical in this company which is growing in size. You see, this is the way people see their way forward - for example, the new Business Unit Manager was the Product Planning Manager for the 9000; he then became the product manager, and now he's head of his own new Business Unit.

Back in the late '60s PERT was all the rage in controlling large project developments. Nowadays we use bar charts, along with other companies like us.

SCORING OF THE HIDDEN STRUCTURES

On the basis of the interview data collected within the John Fluke Manufacturing Company Inc. (relevant excerpts of which have been reported above verbatim), the firm's informal working structures were scored as shown in Tables 5.7 and 5.8.

The Innovative Firms

Table 5.7

FLUKE STRUCTURES FOR INITIATING PRODUCT INNOVATION

1.1   Specialisation

(i)   Do ideas for possible new products stem predominantly from one department, or do several departments involve themselves intimately in this task? (Functional specialisation)

Low	☐	One function only
	☒	Marketing and R&D
High	☐	Marketing, R&D and other(s)

(ii)   By what means do those suggesting ideas get their inspiration? Are any specific activities engaged in - like brainstorming sessions - to increase the potential number of ideas? (Role specialisation)

Low	☐	Ad hoc
	☐	Ad hoc and analytical techniques e.g. lost orders, exhibitions, market surveys
High	☒	Ad hoc and analytical techniques, and regular and formal brainstorming, buzz sessions etc

1.2   Formalisation

(i)   To what extent are those who involve themselves in suggesting ideas for possible new products given guidance or guidelines on this task in writing? (Written guidance)

Low	☒	Not at all
	☐	To some extent
High	☐	Extensively

(ii)   To what extent is information on ideas for possible new products exchanged in writing between those involved? (Written communication)

Low	☒	Predominantly spoken
	☐	More spoken than written
High	☐	More written than spoken

FLUKE STRUCTURES FOR INITIATING PRODUCT INNOVATION continued

1.3   Standardisation

(i)   What guidance is given on the sort of new product ideas the company is seeking? (Consistency in control)

    Low   ☐ Business mission delineated

               ☒ Product market area delineated

    High   ☐ Product area delineated

(ii) How frequently are formal meetings held at which suggestions for possible new products are discussed? (Frequency of reviews)

    Low   ☒ Less frequently than every 3 months

               ☐ At between 1 month and 3 monthly intervals

    High   ☐ Monthly or more frequently

1.4   Centralisation

How much influence does the CEO exert over the flow of ideas for possible new products? (Power retention by CEO)

    Low   ☐ He encourages as many ideas to be put forward as possible - the more the merrier

               ☒ He encourages ideas within the confines of the delineated strategy

    High   ☐ He seeks to keep tight control over the sort of ideas which are put forward

1.5   Stratification

From what level in the organisation are ideas typically taken up? (Seniority of dominant coalition)

    Low   ☒ Departmental executive level

               ☐ H O D level

    High   ☐ Board level

The Innovative Firms

Table 5.8

2. ## FLUKE STRUCTURES FOR IMPLEMENTING PRODUCT INNOVATION

2.1 Specialisation

(i) Which department or departments are intimately involved in the development process? (Functional specialisation)

Low ☐ R&D

☐ Marketing and R&D

High ☒ Marketing, R&D and other(s)

(ii) Certain types of activities can be particularly important in the development process. Do you, for example, have persons who assume responsibility for the following roles? (Role specialisation)

(1) Business/project management (i.e. product championship)
(2) Entrepreneurial interpretation of market trends (market gatekeeping)
(3) Analysis of scientific and engineering trends affecting the development (technical gatekeeping)
(4) Manufacturing/quality gatekeeping
(5) Godfathering (sponsorship by a senior member)

Low ☐ 2 or less roles are specifically provided for

☐ 3-4 roles are specifically provided for

High ☒ All roles are specifically provided for

2.2 Formalisation

(i) In what form are those involved in the development process given guidance or guidelines on their work? (Written guidance)

Low ☐ The process is explained verbally

☐ Some written guidelines are given

High ☒ A control manual is provided

(ii) In what way is progress on specific development tasks noted? (Written communication)

Low ☐ Informal notes are kept

☐ Formal notes are issued as required

High ☒ Formal minutes of meetings are issued

94

FLUKE STRUCTURES FOR IMPLEMENTING PRODUCT INNOVATION continued

2.3   Standardisation

(i)   Are the same development criteria applied to control each project? For example, has each project an equal chance of being stopped? (Consistency in control)

    Low   ☐ Totally different criteria

               ☐ Somewhat different criteria

    High   ☒ Essentially similar criteria

(ii)   How frequently is progress on development work monitored formally? (Frequency of reviews)

    Low   ☐ Less frequently than every 3 months

               ☐ At between 1 month and 3 monthly intervals

    High   ☒ Monthly or more frequently

2.4   Centralisation

    What control or influence does the CEO exert over the development work? (Power retention by CEO)

    Low   ☐ He expects others to get on with it independently

               ☐ He is kept in touch with progress

    High   ☒ He is informed of progress in detail

2.5   Stratification

    At what level is responsibility for the overall success of a project development assumed i.e. at whom is the finger pointed if something goes wrong? (Seniority of dominant coalition)

    Low   ☐ Department executive level

               ☐ H O D level

    High   ☒ Board level

The Innovative Firms

SUMMARY

We see in the case of this firm how efficient
product development can flourish within a fairly
centralised system of control. Just as in the case
of the HP instrument division, a tightly controlled
and coordinated system for monitoring approved
projects follows a much more open method for
encouraging ideas for possible development. Indeed,
there are remarkable similarities between the way HP
monitors product development proper and the way it
is monitored at Fluke, which reflects the diffusion
of good practice.
An important difference between the two firms,
as far as the formal organisation is concerned, is
that Fluke uses Product Planning Managers to
initiate product innovation, whilst HP expects its
Product Marketing Managers to look after both
existing and new products. The chief advantage of
Fluke's system would appear to be that product
planners are immediately available to coordinate the
new product development, and if successful, they can
expect to become its manager. In this way the new
product is assured of an immediate champion.
Another interesting feature of Fluke's procedures for initiating product innovation is the early
involvement of customers in testing a new product in
concept. Many firms, particularly in the instrument
industry, are obsessively secretive about all
aspects of product innovation. Whilst novel
technical solutions must obviously be guarded with
the greatest care, there would appear to be every
advantage in using one's existing and potential
customer base as a method for assessing the type of
technical features which are most needed. Such
practice has considerable advantages over the 'next
bench syndrome' where development engineers look for
inspiration primarily from their close technical
colleagues.

DATRON ELECTRONICS LTD

A description of this company's operations has been included because it shows that efficient product innovation is certainly not the province solely of larger firms. Datron Electronics Ltd was established in 1971 and in the early 1980s employed over 100 people in Norwich, England. The case illustrates particularly the importance attached to 'up front analysis' i.e. the thorough testing of a new product idea in concept, in market and current technical terms. It also illustrates how best practice is transferred from firms, such as Hewlett-Packard, through the movement of key personnel.

BACKGROUND

Datron International Limited, the holding company of Datron Electronics Ltd, was established by Geoffrey Cannell and John Pickering. The former had worked as a technical salesman with a number of instrument companies including Hewlett-Packard and what is now Racal-Dana. In Racal-Dana Cannell became Director of European Operations. John Pickering initially joined Hewlett-Packard and then Racal-Dana.

According to many industry experts, in the late 1960s, the instrument arm of the British company Racal assumed some of the features of a sales-led company by diversifying widely into digital voltmeters (DVMs) and into other product markets which were not closely related in marketing and technical terms. Ultimately this was to lead to a period of retrenchment on the part of the instrument arm of Racal. At the end of the 1960s Solartron was another major British manufacturer of DVMs, but with a product range which was criticised by many at the time as lacking in accuracy.

It was Cannell who initially recognised a potentially profitable gap in the UK DVM market. In 1970 Pickering left Racal-Dana to start manufacturing products similar to DVMs in a garage in Lowestoft to meet the demand of British Aerospace in testing the Rapier missile. The product was a specialised low-frequency true RMS measurement instrument. This was to be the start of Datron's operations, and because the instrument offered a new way of measuring (using a logarithmic conversion technique) it was technically innovative. Indeed, it is to this day on the Datron product range. In 1971 Cannell joined Pickering and the new company started trading. The logarithmic conversion technique has since been adopted by other manufacturers of DVMs, but Datron claims that its instruments are now the most accurate on the market as a result of their accumulated experience.

Expansion of DVM manufacture occurred after 1973 as a reputation was acquired for accuracy and reliability over products then available from firms such as Solartron and certain US suppliers. Multimeters were added to the product range and trading was widened to include Europe. Both product ranges were based on essentially the same manufacturing technology. In 1975 it was decided to supplement the company's product range with products which were equal, if not superior, to those offered by HP, Fluke, Racal-Dana and Solartron. A decision was taken to design these new products with a style appealing to both US and European customers, i.e. to give them a 'mid-atlantic' appearance, in readiness for sales to the US. The new DVM product range launched in 1978 was based on MPU analytical power which enhanced measuring ability. The new range was given the name "Autocal". In 1981 this range of new products won the company a Queen's Award for Technological Innovation (an award introduced in 1975 to recognise and encourage achievements in process or product innovation in British industry).

In 1978 a managing director was recruited with a background of instrument sales in Solartron and latterly with HP. In 1979 the company adopted the overall control structure shown in Table 5.9 which is intended to facilitate expansion into new areas of operations, each headed by a MD with a 10% equity share. In the early 1980s Datron Electronics Ltd accounted for some 80% of group turnover and profits.

Table 5.9

DATRON EXECUTIVE CONTROL STRUCTURE

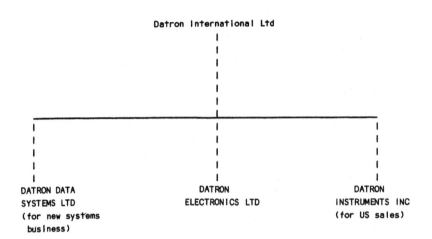

Datron International Ltd

| DATRON DATA SYSTEMS LTD (for new systems business) | DATRON ELECTRONICS LTD | DATRON INSTRUMENTS INC (for US sales) |

The philosophy underpinning the overall control structure is to allow semi-autonomous operating companies to be established. When a particular company reaches a certain size the intention is to split its operations, either into divisions or totally, so that a relatively flat management structure can be maintained for communications purposes. (It must be remembered that the principal officers have had experience of the 'HP way' and, indeed, admire and wish to emulate it in their own organisation). A separate company has been set up to expand sales in the US, a market which is perceived to account for one-half of the world's potential for the company's current products.

99

THE FORMAL STRUCTURE

As is usual in innovative instrument manufacturing firms the latest version of the formal organisation chart is out of date. The Managing Director described the present organisation, depicted in Table 5.10 as follows:

> Our management style is undoubtedly informal. We do not have a lot of memo writing. We are still small enough that we can communicate with all employees and we have a meeting every month of all employees for about half an hour when we review briefly our successes and failures for the month. Usually the meeting takes the form of a presentation by one of the senior managers. The management are generally friends as well as colleagues, so a lot of discussion takes place outside usual office hours. We are keen that anybody can speak to anybody in the company. We are all on first name terms and we operate the open-door approach. As in Hewlett - Packard, we all wear name badges.

> I act both as MD and Marketing Director. We do not have a Personnel Manager because of our compact size. I take responsibility for that function and the administration is carried out by my secretary. Also, it's important to remember that everyone here is directly responsible for their own personnel. We believe in that very, very strongly. We would not want a Personnel Director, although in time we shall need a Personnel Manager. I believe personnel is advisory only. As in HP, and in other US companies, we believe departmental heads need to take responsibility for their staff.

> The Product Marketing Manager is a new position to balance the R&D strength of the company. Ultimately, he will have Product Managers under him, who will look after the marketing of products in the range.

Table 5.10

ORGANISATION CHART - DATRON ELECTRONICS LTD

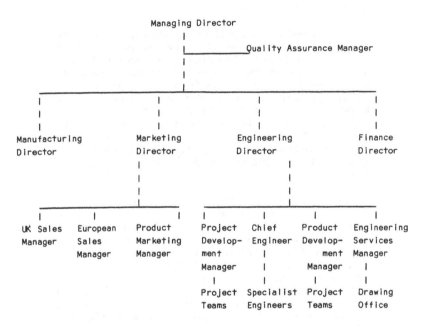

Engineering Director:

The way I fit into the organisation is
fairly complex because I was one of the
founder members. Recently, I have
restructured Engineering to split product
development tasks into two: one part
dealing with the initiation of new
development. This task is coordinated by
a Project Development Manager. You can
see from the the chart (Table 5.11) that
it is his job to get an idea for a
possible new product into the shape of
what we call a Product Feasibility Report.
No, he is not just an ideas man, he will
be required to explore the technical
feasibility of developing particular
circuits on which the new product would

101

be reliant. Essentially, though, the job
of the Project Development Manager is to
get the idea hardened out so that we can
assess its likelihood of technical and
commercial success.

Once a Product Feasibility Report has been
approved the responsibility is passed over
to the Product Development Manager and
development work proper begins. Indeed,
most members of a project team concerned
with preparing the Product Feasibility
Report will actually move across to join
the product development team. The
important point is that management
accountability is separated between the
feasibility phase and the development
phase.

I have recently introduced this changed
control structure because we had become
somewhat inefficient on large product
developments. We were concentrating too
much on the product specification without
concentrating on the techniques required
to meet that specification. In other
words, we were getting committed to a
particular product and momentum was built
up based on circuit blocks which did not
always work all that well. This is a
fundamental change in responsibilities.

Additionally, because we have experienced
difficulty in recruiting good technical
people, and also because it is difficult
to assess who is good, I have decided to
appoint heads of specific disciplines
under the direction of the Chief Engineer.
It is from his staff of engineers that the
staff for particular projects is drawn.
In this way we have established a matrix
pattern within the Engineering Department.
At present, I act as Chief Engineer, but
this will change as the company grows. We
can now assess not only whether engineers
are working hard, but also their technical
competence.

The change in organisation structure
reflects our wish to introduce more

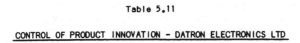

Table 5.11

CONTROL OF PRODUCT INNOVATION - DATRON ELECTRONICS LTD

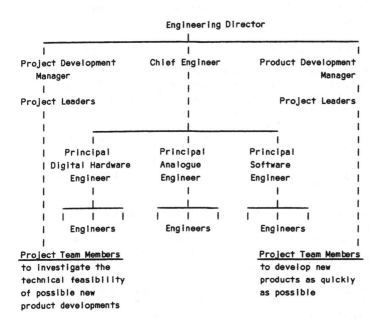

control into the product development process. We will now get hardware and software designs signed-off at appropriate stages of a product's development; previously this was done only prior to production, when it was too late and caused too many delays. This is important, because in a matrix structure responsibilities are not defined very precisely, which requires one to formalise the actions or results required.

Clearly, the Project Development Manager will have close interest in the markets at present being served by the Product Marketing Manager, and in this respect they will be in close touch with each other. It is the specific task of the

103

Project Development Manager to go out to talk with customers. Essentially, he is an explorer of ideas for possible new products, yet he has the technical expertise to conceptualise these market needs in product terms.

I once worked in a company in which specifications were put forward solely by Marketing. If it had been a true marketing department, it might have worked. But what happened was that specifications were being put forward which identified features on which orders had been lost in the last sale. No one was doing any fundamental innovative thinking on technical grounds. This meant that the company began to chase the competition rather than to lead.

Essentially, now, I am trying to keep the whole of the Engineering Department close to the market-place. I never want to see the day when Marketing sends us a definitive product specification - that's the way to close your eyes to alternative opportunities. You are then in danger of solely reacting to competitors rather than taking the initiative and leading.

THE HIDDEN STRUCTURES

For initiating product innovation

Managing Director:

In the case of an existing product line the initiative would come from Marketing in general terms. Input on the feasibility of meeting such marketing requirements will then come from Engineering.

In the case of a completely new market opportunity, to be met by a new class of product, it is just as likely that the initiative will stem from R&D . It might, however, come from somewhere else - QA for instance, or Manufacturing.

Yes, we do have brainstorming sessions. About every 3 months we lock the management group away for 1 or 2 days in a hotel to discuss many topics. Often new product ideas will be tossed around at these meetings and frequently outsiders are invited to attend. If the discussion is on specific new product opportunities we will have along some quite junior engineers. The whole idea is to loosen-up from our day-to-day responsibilies at these meetings.

When we are back here there is nothing to stop someone with an idea for a possible new product sending a memo about it, but generally it will first be kicked-around verbally. The initiator might then be invited to put it in writing so that more people might consider it.

When we need to update products within an existing product range then management does give engineers and others direction. However, we try to keep the whole philosophy open, so that anyone can come along with ideas to someone at a senior level. This is important, because the whole structure of the parent company is designed to allow us to set up business units which do not fit with current operations. Generally, however, we are clear in the shorter run about the sort of new product ideas we are looking for – they are for premium test instruments for systems use.

For evaluating alternatives

Managing Director:

We don't have a formal checklist. ROI is important. The marketplace is very important, by that I mean we must have experience of selling the new product. It needs to fit in with our current marketing expertise. Then it must fit in with our manufacturing capability – ours is for low-batch quality instruments.

Engineering Director:

> As has been mentioned, every quarter we assess the strategic posture of the company at a weekend away in an hotel. But we also go away as a senior management team to exhibitions, where ideas are stimulated, particularly when we are in California in the States. Don't forget that strategy formulation in a company of our size is rather informal.

For implementing product innovation

Engineering Director:

> Historically, we have incurred 5-7% of total development expenses up to the time a Product Feasibility Report has been submitted. What I believe we should be doing is to incur nearer 20%. I am pretty sure that if we double the earlier expenditure we will be able to halve our later product development expenditures. That's good gearing. We have not in the past put nearly enough effort, in my opinion, at the front-end.

> Specifically, I want to see the ideas and technical concepts associated with a possible new product explored and tested in far greater detail. By involving more people earlier I want our Product Feasibility Reports to be more realistic. It is this which I am aiming at with our new engineering organisation structure.

> During the product development process proper there is some involvement by just about every department of the company. Even the Finance Department might be looking for DOI grants. In practice, however, it is mainly Marketing and R&D. Manufacturing does get involved, but it's small at the moment, because we don't have a formal Production Engineering function. QA also gets involved.

Yes, we always appoint a project leader
for a sizeable development. Yes, I am an
important market gatekeeper as you call
him. The project leader also does this.
Quality gate-keeping is provided for under
my new matrix structure. No, we don't do
what you call godfathering – I guess
that's more appropriate to reluctant
bureaucracies.

We do not, at the moment, have sufficient
written checkpoints in our development
processes. Nor do we have sufficient
written guidance. As I have said, I am
working on these at the moment – they will
be out and working quite soon. What you
have listed 'High' under Formalisation,
Standardisation, and Stratification will
all be met shortly. There is going to be a
series of documents and reviews which will
require approval to go beyond specific
development points. Until now we have
really only had one, which has been the
initial Product Feasibility Report. This
has been a product spec based on very
little technical knowledge... and given
the 'Go' at that point, a project has gone
on for ever under its own volition... that
is something management needs to control
much better. We did also have an
Engineering Model Review, but that was too
far along the development path – and by
the time we had something good enough to
be called an engineering model the product
development had picked up too much steam
to stop it ... and anyway, the sales
department was expecting it shortly! No,
at present we don't have formal
checkpoints, but soon we will have them.

No, we do not formally review product
developments monthly. Whether we should
or not I am not sure....not sure....I
think I would rather do it by event.
Unless there are exceptions, I would
rather look at programmes separately at
event points. The reason why I say this is
that I want to focus on these as essential
control points. A regular monthly meeting
sounds too mechanistic for my liking.

The Innovative Firms

Managing Director:

I suppose as we get bigger and get more
programmes under way we may have to have
monthly meetings at which these are all
monitored.

Engineering Director:

Coming back to what I was saying - I am
very keen to focus on particular event
points. I would head such meetings, the MD
would be invited to attend, as would all
the interested parties. I would see such a
meeting being a major event of a very
formal nature.

SCORING OF THE HIDDEN STRUCTURES

On the basis of the interview data collected
within Datron Electronics Ltd (relevant excerpts of
which have been reported above verbatim), the firm's
working structures were scored as shown in Tables
5.12 and 5.13.

Table 5.12

DATRON STRUCTURES FOR INITIATING PRODUCT INNOVATION

1.1   Specialisation

(i)   Do ideas for possible new products stem predominantly from one department, or do several departments involve themselves intimately in this task? (Functional specialisation)

     Low   ☐ One function only

               ☒ Marketing and R&D

     High   ☐ Marketing, R&D and other(s)

(ii)   By what means do those suggesting ideas get their inspiration? Are any specific activities engaged in – like brainstorming sessions – to increase the potential number of ideas? (Role specialisation)

     Low   ☐ Ad hoc

               ☒ Ad hoc and analytical techniques
                   e.g. lost orders, exhibitions, market surveys

     High   ☐ Ad hoc and analytical techniques, and regular and
                   formal brainstorming, buzz sessions etc

1.2   Formalisation

(i)   To what extent are those who involve themselves in suggesting ideas for possible new products given guidance or guidelines on this task in writing? (Written guidance)

     Low   ☒ Not at all

               ☐ To some extent

     High   ☐ Extensively

(ii)   To what extent is information on ideas for possible new products exchanged in writing between those involved? (Written communication)

     Low   ☒ Predominantly spoken

               ☐ More spoken than written

     High   ☐ More written than spoken

The Innovative Firms

1.3   Standardisation

(i)   What guidance is given on the sort of new product ideas the company is seeking? (Consistency in control)

Low	☐	Business mission delineated
	☒	Product market area delineated
High	☐	Product area delineated

(ii)   How frequently are formal meetings held at which suggestions for possible new products are discussed? (Frequency of reviews)

Low	☒	Less frequently than every 3 months
	☐	At between 1 month and 3 monthly intervals
High	☐	Monthly or more frequently

1.4   Centralisation

How much influence does the CEO exert over the flow of ideas for possible new products? (Power retention by CEO)

Low	☐	He encourages as many ideas to be put forward as possible - the more the merrier
	☒	He encourages ideas within the confines of the delineated strategy
High	☐	He seeks to keep tight control over the sort of ideas which are put forward

1.5   Stratification

From what level in the organisation are ideas typically taken up? (Seniority of dominant coalition)

Low	☒	Departmental executive level
	☐	H O D level
High	☐	Board level

110

Table 5.13

2.   DATRON STRUCTURES FOR IMPLEMENTING PRODUCT INNOVATION

2.1   Specialisation

(i)   Which department or departments are intimately involved in the development process? (Functional specialisation)

Low   ☐ R&D

             ☐ Marketing and R&D

High   ☒ Marketing, R&D and other(s)

(ii) Certain types of activities can be particularly important in the development process. Do you, for example, have persons who assume responsibility for the following roles? (Role specialisation)

(1)   Business/project management (i.e. product championship)
(2)   Entrepreneurial interpretation of market trends (market gatekeeping)
(3)   Analysis of scientific and engineering trends affecting the development (technical gatekeeping)
(4)   Manufacturing/quality gatekeeping
(5)   Godfathering (sponsorship by a senior member)

Low   ☐ 2 or less roles are specifically provided for

             ☐ 3-4 roles are specifically provided for

High   ☒ All roles are specifically provided for

2.2   Formalisation

(i)   In what form are those involved in the development process given guidance or guidelines on their work? (Written guidance)

Low   ☐ The process is explained verbally

             ☒ Some written guidelines are given

High   ☐ A control manual is provided

(ii) In what way is progress on specific development tasks noted? (Written communication)

Low   ☐ Informal notes are kept

             ☒ Formal notes are issued as required

High   ☐ Formal minutes of meetings are issued

The Innovative Firms

2.3   Standardisation

(i)   Are the same development criteria applied to control each project? For
example, has each project an equal chance of being stopped? (consistency in
control)

      Low   ☐ Totally different criteria

                ☒ Somewhat different criteria

      High   ☐ Essentially similar criteria

(ii)   How frequently is progress on development work monitored formally?
(Frequency of reviews)

      Low   ☐ Less frequently than every 3 months

                ☒ At between 1 month and 3 monthly intervals

      High   ☐ Monthly or more frequently

2.4   Centralisation

What control or influence does the CEO exert over the development work?
(Power retention by CEO)

      Low   ☐ He expects others to get on with it independently

                ☐ He is kept in touch with progress

      High   ☒ He is informed of progress in detail

2.5   Stratification

At what level is responsibility for the overall success of a project
development assumed i.e. at whom is the finger pointed if something goes
wrong? (Seniority of dominant coalition)

      Low   ☐ Department executive level

                ☐ H O D level

      High   ☒ Board level

112

SUMMARY

We see how in this relatively small firm great importance is attached to exploring ideas for possible new products in concept. Whereas in the Fluke case the responsibility for this task was vested in the marketing department with (new) Product Planning Managers, in the case of this small firm the responsibility is undertaken by the engineering department. Asked whether the reason for this decision had been taken because there is not, as yet, a formally established marketing function in Datron Electronics Ltd., the Engineering Director replied:

> In part, yes, but there is another reason why I have introduced the above changes. I have seen a situation in a company I used to work where it failed abysmally because the Sales Department led everything. No one expected the Engineering Department to put forward ideas for new products.

No doubt as Datron Electronics continues to grow a marketing function will be established formally, after which it will be possible for product innovation to be initiated jointly between engineering and marketing. As far as implementation activities are concerned, the Engineering Director is currently developing a control schema incorporating specific milestones at which project progress will have to be 'signed-off' by those concerned.

Chapter Six

HOW LESS INNOVATIVE FIRMS ORGANISE

     This chapter describes how three less
experienced product innovator firms approach the
problems associated with bringing new products to
market. What methods are in place for this purpose,
as in Chapter 5, are again described predominantly
in the words of the persons who are involved. Each
case illustrates the problems faced by firms with
little or no experience of regular and speedy
product innovation. The last case, which follows a
slightly different pattern, demonstrates the risks
inherent in undertaking little or no product innovation over a lengthy period of time. To respect
confidences, the contents of all cases are disguised
in order to protect the innocent, as well as those
guilty of having neglected product innovation in the
past.

COLONIAL INSTRUMENTS LTD

     This case is of interest because it illustrates
the problems faced by firms which have relied for
too long on old-established 'cash cow' products.
Such a situation is most likely to arise in older
established firms and particularly in those where
the founder or his surviving family members exert a
stultifying influence on product innovation. The
case illustrates the special problems faced by firms
with little or no experience of product innovation.

114

BACKGROUND

Colonial Instruments Ltd (Colonial) is now part of a large British holding group, having been bought in the early 1970s. The history of Colonial dates back to the 1880s when the founder started manufacturing electrical fittings which were supplied to famous buildings in Britain and Europe. In time the founder's business was to take him into many different types of electrical product markets including instruments. The business prospered throughout the first half of the twentieth century, but in recent years profitability has been much lower than previously.

On being acquired, the diverse activities of Colonial were split, for executive control purposes, into several semi-autonomous operating units. The case investigation concerns itself solely with the activities of the instrument division, which in 1981 employed over 1000 persons. The division – referred for sake of brevity solely as Colonial – today manufactures an extensive range of electro-mechanical indicating and measuring instruments. It does not compete in the very high volume, low price, low accuracy indicating instrument markets such as for automobile dashboards, consumer stereo units or domestic battery chargers. Equally, its products are not aimed at very specialist segments such as flight instrumentation.

The recently appointed Sales Manager summed up the circumstances facing the division in the following words:

> Our company is faced with a major external environmental threat. The market is at the threshold of a period of technological substitution. Competitors have already developed electronic analogue instruments. As is typical, these are currently being sold into high price, low volume market segments. The medical, military and scientific markets are good examples. The trend will be for the price of these higher technology products to decline very rapidly and for sales to gradually encroach into the volume segments of the market.

115

Increasingly in the future, we expect more and more end-users of our products to employ microprocessor technology. Therefore, instrumentation will need to interface with the silicon chip. The signal inputs will not be great enough to drive a traditional electro-mechanical instrument. The market for our company's existing products can, therefore, be expected to decline. Modern process control now employs computers. Microprocessor technology is already being employed to reduce fuel consumption in mass-produced automobiles. Its introduction into our line of products has already started. At a recent exhibition it was noticeable that many of our competitors have responded to these technological changes by offering a number of new electronic products.

I regret to say that our product portfolio is now seriously out of balance. We are dependent on ageing cash cow products. Insufficient effort has been devoted to research and to the development of new products aimed at potential growth markets.

I must stress, however, that our marketing mix does have a number of important strengths. The range of products is extensive. The speed of service is very good. In the UK market, home loyalty and customer familiarity with the Colonial name are advantages. But, and it's a big but, we are continually having to respond to, rather than initiate, price reductions. This is significant, as it implies that aggressive competitors are operating with lower average cost structures.

Sad to say, we do not project an up-market image. We appear reluctant to drop, or at least stop promoting, our old products. In short, our marketing strategy is through necessity to retain a reasonable share of large established markets, primarily on the basis of price competitiveness. In the longer run, it's obvious that we must innovate to survive.

THE FORMAL STRUCTURE

Day-to-day management responsiblity is shared between the seven executives shown in Table 6.1. It has been mentioned that Colonial is now part of a large holding company where it is placed within the Electronics Product Group for control purposes. It is of interest to note that the members of the Electronics Product Group, on which the MD of Colonial sits, meets monthly, whilst the board of Colonial meets only on a three-monthly basis. Several executives commented unfavourably on this organisational arrangement, some even going as far as to describe the formal structure and mode of operation as "a mess". The reader will note that the executive board of Colonial is made up primarily of the General Managers of the separate operating sites, with only scant representation by functional specialists.

Table 6.1

EXECUTIVE CONTROL STRUCTURE - COLONIAL

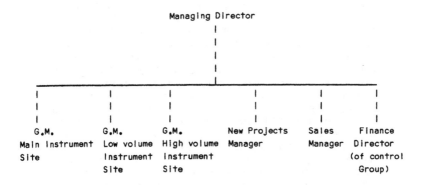

The Less Innovative Firms

It is relevant to mention that the whole of Colonial is pervaded by an old company atmosphere, which manifests itself in an extremely bureaucratic method of communication. For example, memos are addressed to persons not by name; not even by their job title, but by abbreviated job titles. Examples being: MD - Managing Director; SM - Sales Manager, etc. Indeed, every task is carefully documented in this old-established firm and a standard operating system has been established for nearly every decision, except (as was expressed in a cynical joke), the way the firm should be wound-up if it fails to weather the current recession.

THE HIDDEN STRUCTURES

For initiating product innovation

The Sales Manager commented on the firm's current procedures for introducing new products as follows:

> We have no established system. Even when the need for product innovation becomes more widely accepted at the topmost levels of this company, we have yet to face up to the wide range of problems associated with a diversification programme. For many years the company has depended on the sale of low-technology electro-mechanical products into a few closely defined market segments. Because of the relatively slow rate of change in the established technology, the company has operated with very small expenditures on development. Due to our company's long history and the market knowledge built up over many decades, it has not been considered necessary to devote resources to market research, or to the search for new business opportunities outside our established markets. It is true that we have some new products, but these are based on technology and designs which have been copied, and so far we have only marketed two new products. Unfortunately, it is as yet unclear what the precise markets are for these new products.

When asked how ideas for possible new products are collected the Chief Engineer remarked:

We have been in the measuring game for nearly one hundred years. I was recruited to simplify the design of instruments because over the last 20 years it has become increasingly difficult to get the skilled labour required to make really intricate electro-mechanical products. One way to overcome this problem has been to incorporate transducers in our instruments which convert AC input into DC output, which can then be shown on a relatively simple electro-mechanical moving coil indicator.

Our 500 series (the only recent new product) grew out of these changes in production technology. After having overcome the labour difficulties through incorporating transducers into our instruments, we became aware that a market existed for such devices for feeding information into a wider range of indicating instruments, such as data loggers for example, which are used by public utilities for monitoring the generation of electricity at remote locations. The problem with meeting this wider demand was that utilities such as Area Boards insisted on tight specifications. It was really their insistence on particular specifications which permits us to call the 500 series a new product range. Prior to that, it was merely a product which we manufactured for incorporation into our own products but which we were prepared to sell when a customer asked for it.

For evaluating alternatives

Asked how the 500 series had been selected for eventual development the Chief Engineer replied:

It would be fairer to say that the 500 series evolved rather than it having been purposively developed as a new product range. I don't think that at any particular

time did we say that we needed to do this or
that - it was just that the demands of big
users like the utilities over the last 3 to
4 years forced us gradually to improve the
specifications. It was in this way that the
new product was born, and we are now trying
to sell it to a wider market.

For Implementing product innovation

When asked who was involved in actually
developing the new product, the Chief Engineer
remarked:

It was a very loose group of persons who
were involved. At the time there was a chap
who joined us from another firm who had been
very much involved in working with
utilities. In fact, the utilities and his
previous firm had worked very closely
together in the manufacture of transducers.
The man who joined us used to be a sales
manager there and had been closely involved
in producing transducers which met the
specifications laid down by the utilities.
He was able to guide us a little bit as far
as packaging (designing) our new product was
concerned.

Asked whether the "newcomer" had taken charge of
the new product's development, the Chief Engineer
replied:

No, he was in charge of the sales side, but
it's difficult to say . . . we have been
very loose in the past with this sort of
thing. It was my job to get the design work
going and to get the tests done to see that
the utilities' specifications were met. I
did this along with other work I had going
on at the time.

I had a small group - one electronics design
engineer, one electronics trainee on it
part-time, one draughtsman and some part-
time help to get the new transducer ready
for the market. As soon as we began selling
the new range we got orders for types of

transducers which we had not, as yet
designed. This meant that the design work
was actually happening after we had sold
them!

Asked whether anyone in particular had taken
charge of the product's development the Chief
Engineer replied:

We used to have meetings . . . but no one
in particular was in charge . . . in the
past with all new products we have never had
a laid down plan or someone as leader. It
was nearly always left to me. It has been
me who pointed out that we needed to do
something about a product not selling very
well; if it was difficult to make, or if it
didn't quite meet what customers wanted.
This information will have come to my notice
by way of complaints from customers and
complaints from area sales managers, and so
gradually I would form an opinion that the
product required some attention. So we
would do something about it, and hopefully
it would sell better after that.

We did, in fact, have some product
development meetings. The MD used to take
the chair, I think, in those. Usually the
Sales Manager would join us, someone from
production would be there, and there would
be someone from accounts. So I suppose we
did have some sort of committee, but it was
very loose. The meetings were a bit erratic
- every 3 or 4 weeks. The MD would call the
meetings. We all hoped he would not call
them because normally the job was moving
along as fast as it could and fresh ideas
thrown in at meetings would usually slow it
. . . he used to call meetings to find out
what was going on. None of these projects
had anyone in particular in charge of them,
but the MD saw it as his job to keep an
overall eye on what was happening.

Asked how money was allocated to develop a new
product the Chief Engineer replied:

None of the new products have ever been

formally funded. We have always had to find
the development resources somehow out of
slack. When I was with my previous firm,
where I also ran a design department, I was
allowed to spend X% of company turnover on
design. Typically, I would spend that on
new products rather than on the existing
products.

Here, as you know, most of our low-
technology production has been moved to
another site to capitalise on lower labour
costs. Normally, one would expect money
made on sales to fund the development costs
of new products. This has not happened . .
this difficulty in funding means that some
2 years after launching the new 500 series
we are still working on odds and ends to do
with development aspects.

SCORING OF THE HIDDEN STRUCTURES

On the basis of the interview data collected
within Colonial Instruments Ltd (relevant excerpts
of which have been reported above verbatim), the
firm's informal working structures were scored as
shown in Tables 6.2 and 6.3

Table 6.2

COLONIAL STRUCTURES FOR INITIATING PRODUCT INNOVATION

1.1 Specialisation

(i) Do ideas for possible new products stem predominantly from one department, or do several departments involve themselves intimately in this task? (Functional specialisation)

Low   [X]   One function only

             [ ]   Marketing and R&D

High   [ ]   Marketing, R&D and other(s)

(ii) By what means do those suggesting ideas get their inspiration? Are any specific activities engaged in - like brainstorming sessions - to increase the potential number of ideas? (Role specialisation)

Low   [X]   Ad hoc

             [ ]   Ad hoc and analytical techniques
                   e.g. lost orders, exhibitions, market surveys

High   [ ]   Ad hoc and analytical techniques, and regular and
                   formal brainstorming, buzz sessions etc

1.2 Formalisation

(i) To what extent are those who involve themselves in suggesting ideas for possible new products given guidance or guidelines on this task in writing? (Written guidance)

Low   [X]   Not at all

             [ ]   To some extent

High   [ ]   Extensively

(ii) To what extent is information on ideas for possible new products exchanged in writing between those involved? (Written communication)

Low   [ ]   Predominantly spoken

             [ ]   More spoken than written

High   [X]   More written than spoken

The Less Innovative Firms

1.3   Standardisation

(i)   What guidance is given on the sort of new product ideas the company is seeking? (Consistency in control)

    Low   ☐   Business mission delineated

                   ☐   Product market area delineated

    High   ☒   Product area delineated

(ii)   How frequently are formal meetings held at which suggestions for possible new products are discussed? (Frequency of reviews)

    Low   ☒   Less frequently than every 3 months

                   ☐   At between 1 month and 3 monthly intervals

    High   ☐   Monthly or more frequently

1.4   Centralisation

    How much influence does the CEO exert over the flow of ideas for possible new products? (Power retention by CEO)

    Low   ☐   He encourages as many ideas to be put forward as possible - the more the merrier

                   ☐   He encourages ideas within the confines of the delineated strategy

    High   ☒   He seeks to keep tight control over the sort of ideas which are put forward

1.5   Stratification

    From what level in the organisation are ideas typically taken up? (Seniority of dominant coalition)

    Low   ☒   Departmental executive level

                   ☐   H O D level

    High   ☐   Board level

Table 6.3

COLONIAL STRUCTURES FOR IMPLEMENTING PRODUCT INNOVATION

2.1   Specialisation

(i)   Which department or departments are intimately involved in the development process? (Functional specialisation)

Low   [X] R&D

          [ ] Marketing and R&D

High   [ ] Marketing, R&D and other(s)

(ii) Certain types of activities can be particularly important in the development process.   Do you, for example, have persons who assume responsibility for the following roles? (Role specialisation)

(1)   Business/project management (i.e. product championship)
(2)   Entrepreneurial interpretation of market trends (market gatekeeping)
(3)   Analysis of scientific and engineering trends affecting the development (technical gatekeeping)
(4)   Manufacturing/quality gatekeeping
(5)   Godfathering (sponsorship by a senior member)

Low   [X] 2 or less roles are specifically provided for

          [ ] 3-4 roles are specifically provided for

High   [ ] All roles are specifically provided for

2.2   Formalisation

(i)   In what form are those involved in the development process given guidance or guidelines on their work? (Written guidance)

Low   [X] The process is explained verbally

          [ ] Some written guidelines are given

High   [ ] A control manual is provided

(ii) In what way is progress on specific development tasks noted? (Written communication)

Low   [X] Informal notes are kept

          [ ] Formal notes are issued as required

High   [ ] Formal minutes of meetings are issued

The Less Innovative Firms

2.3   Standardisation

(i)   Are the same development criteria applied to control each project? For example, has each project an equal chance of being stopped? (Consistency in control)

Low   ☒ Totally different criteria

          ☐ Somewhat different criteria

High   ☐ Essentially similar criteria

(ii)   How frequently is progress on development work monitored formally? (Frequency of reviews)

Low   ☐ Less frequently than every 3 months

          ☒ At between 1 month and 3 monthly intervals

High   ☐ Monthly or more frequently

2.4   Centralisation

What control or influence does the CEO exert over the development work? (Power retention by CEO)

Low   ☐ He expects others to get on with it independently

          ☒ He is kept in touch with progress

High   ☐ He is informed of progress in detail

2.5   Stratification

At what level is responsibility for the overall success of a project development assumed i.e. at whom is the finger pointed if something goes wrong? (Seniority of dominant coalition)

Low   ☒ Department executive level

          ☐ H O D level

High   ☐ Board level

SUMMARY

The predicament in which this firm finds itself
has been well summarised by the Sales Manager:

There are very great difficulties in
shifting a company from dependence on one
technology. In most cases technological
diversification is expensive and requires
considerable funding. At present we are
faced with the typical chicken and egg
dilemma. Which markets offer opportunities
and what are the technical specifications of
the products needed to exploit particular
identified markets? How can we answer these
questions with so little in-house knowledge
of either the markets or of the technology
associated with new products? How can the
company justify the funding of market
research and information, and of building up
the desired technical skills and expertise
in the absence of firm proposals about the
product markets which we intend to exploit?
But I don't think this dilemma is unique to
our company. The problem is faced by every
company when the dominant product approaches
the maturity stage of its life cycle.

SALINE INSTRUMENTS LTD

This case is of interest because it illustrates the sort of problems likely to be faced by a firm which has made itself unduly dependent upon a few major customers. It is shown how these problems can affect even a firm with a very wide product range, particularly when technical expertise is not balanced with marketing expertise.

BACKGROUND

Saline Instruments was one of the founder companies of a group that was later to be merged into one of Britain's larger electrical and electronic conglomerates. Although the firm is nominally placed within a particular control group of the parent company it is allowed considerable freedom to pursue its own course. Within the parent company Saline is regarded as a useful cash cow, which in 1982 employed over 1000 persons.

Saline manufactures both component products and instruments. Margins on components have in recent years been seriously eroded, hence top management now places emphasis on developing the instrument side of the business.

The Managing Director described the present operation as follows:

> About half of our total output goes to the Post Office [now British Telecom] or to export markets which have been determined by the Post Office. So you see, the Post Office occupies a very important position in our marketing strategy. However, the amount we are doing for the [National] Coal Board is tending to increase. After all, we have been doing work for them using radiation measurement of some sort or other for a long time now so we have built up some expertise. This led us to develop techniques for steering coal-cutting machines, and now there is quite a large export market for these. It's really a monitoring, display

and control system, into which we have just recently built a microprocessor. Over the next few years we shall develop this to give increased facilities to coal-cutting operators.

In the case of the Post Office business, it's the sort of moving iron meters you saw in the works which we sell to them. More recently, they have asked us to do some signal processing instrumentation for them. This is a new type of equipment which we are keeping under wraps at the moment.

In terms of volume growth for our current product range: the loading coil market is dying and the rectifier market is dying, the coil winding market is increasing; the instrument market is static at the moment; the electronics market is increasing; the thermostat market has declined because of the slump in the white goods market; the capacitor market is increasing. That basically covers all our products. All in all, our markets are about level-pegging . . ... so, if you want to show year-by-year expansion, you have got problems, haven't you?

A lot of our old markets are disappearing quite rapidly, that's why half our current R&D and marketing effort is aimed at new markets with new products. But unfortunately, we are only able to spend 2% of our present sales turnover on R&D. You see we are losing, in volume terms, about 15% of our product range every year. By this I mean the demand for 15% of our products is falling away every year. These products need to be replaced. You see, we need to spend a certain amount on R&D just to stand still. Any expansion comes on top of that. Unfortunately, at the present time, the market is so dead in many areas that it is extremely difficult to see where expansion can come from.

At one time we had a bigger demand than we could ever supply. Although prices were

tight, they were not as tight as they are
now. We are now suddenly facing competition
from abroad at very much reduced prices.
Many prices are 20% lower this year than
they were last year . . . we either try to
follow these prices down, or we go out of
business. In trying to meet the lower
prices we are having to spend a great deal
of engineering effort on existing products,
when really it should be being spent on
developing new products. This is not so in
all areas, but is certainly so in
thermostats, capacitors and it's beginning
to be so with certain instruments where we
are getting competitors coming in from the
Far East. We do have developments afoot to
combat this competition with new generations
of instruments with cheaper movements, but
it's going to take several years to bring
these in.

All this means, in my opinion, that we are
spending R&D on the wrong sort of things,
but we have got to face up to the fact that
unless we bring in the pound notes next
year, there is not going to be a business
left.

THE FORMAL STRUCTURE

A formal organisation chart is published and
made available to all employees. As is often the
case in older firms the structure is complex and
steeped in the history of power struggles between
individuals and between departments. It is
reproduced in Table 6.4. The Production Director
(who also acts as Assistant Managing Director)
explained the formal organisation as follows:

A product manager in our company manages the
product . . . production planning; profit
and loss on product lines. He is not
responsible for developments on his
products. For that we have separate
laboratory areas, which come under the
control of the Technical Director. Each
laboratory area has an engineering manager

in charge. The R&D budget is split between these laboratory areas.

Table 6.4

EXECUTIVE CONTROL STRUCTURE - SALINE

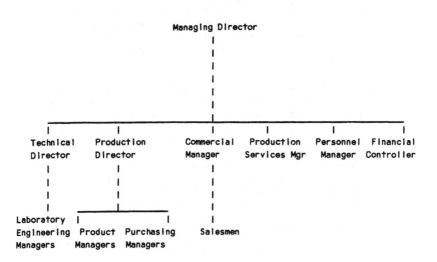

New products are handed over to the product manager when the laboratories have cleared with the Production Services Manager that the product development is ready to go into production. The product manager then chairs a little meeting with the Technical Director, the head of the lab and the Production Services Manager to acquaint him with what is required to launch the product. Normally, after the new product has been launched, the lab will back out . . . but because the new products we are developing now are tending to become more complex the lab interest often continues for longer than the handover to production.

131

The Less Innovative Firms

THE HIDDEN STRUCTURES

For initiating product innovation

Technical Director:

> Quite a lot of our work is sponsored from
> outside - mainly the Post Office or the Coal
> Board - particularly the latter. The
> advantage of this sort of work is that (i)
> at the end of the day you have a ready
> market for it, and (ii) we can keep abreast
> of advancing technology at someone else's
> expense.

> No, we don't tend to tell our customers
> about new products. In the case of the Post
> Office, they almost invariably know what
> they want, so they tell us what they
> require. The same happens in the case of
> British Gas: they tell us what they want
> and we develop it generally at our expense.
> As far as the Coal Board is concerned they
> pay us for what they want and they tell us
> what they want, but in their case they also
> respond to us suggesting things to them. I
> would say 25% of the work we do for the Coal
> Board is at our suggestion, probably based
> on things we have done for them before or
> have noticed generally; the other 75% is
> what they want and they ask us to quote for.

> Don't forget that a very important part of
> our development work is not necessarily
> producing a completely new product but in
> reinforcing it . . . to make it easier to
> make or to make it cheaper. In fact, about
> half the development work we do is that sort
> of [process] innovation.

Laboratory Engineering Manager:

> Ideas for possible new products come from a
> multitude of sources but mainly from within
> the technical function and then it's usually
> up to someone at my level to do something
> about them. If I think it's a good idea I
> will allow people to spend some time on

132

developing the idea further. If the idea then continues to show promise I will then pass it on to the Technical Director.

Ideas do occasionally get suggested by the sales people, but I would get to hear about these through the Technical Director, who feeds them down to me, as it were . . . As we discussed over lunch our so-called marketing managers are really sales people and we treat them as such. If there are any technical aspects to be discussed with a customer, then a technical man has to go along. It is us who get information back from customers, frequently before the marketing people do.

Ideas for possible new products are predominantly ad hoc . . we only use brainstorming sessions to solve particular customer needs. Occasionally marketing people try to increase the flow of ideas for possible new products, but it usually ends up with us giving them reasons why they will not work . . Initially we like to get ideas down in writing . . We don't need frequent formal meetings on ideas - we are tossing these around all the time.

You will gather that at Saline technical staff are not too pleased with the marketing function. This is not limited to us alone. That's why we quite often get information from customers prior to it being fed to marketing. Don't forget, it is we who are dealing with our customers' engineering staff, and they are more likely to talk to us about their problems than they are with their own purchasing officers. Our customers' engineers can talk to us in their own language. This has meant that quite often we have agreed a technical specification with our opposite numbers in the engineering department, which is then passed to their purchasing people to pass to our marketing people. I suppose in some ways it is wrong to bypass the system in this way, but it frequently happens. You can see, therefore, why we have a somewhat low opinion of our marketing people.

I admire those German companies where the head man understands all the technology and expects this of his staff also. I have met a lot of British marketing people, both in this company and in the firms we sell our equipment to, and they all seem to fall into the same mould . . . very personable, but insufficiently briefed on the technical details. This is a real problem because the more complex the technology becomes, the more technically qualified we shall want our marketing people to be in the future.

Evaluation of alternatives

Technical Director:

We work to a three year plan which is updated every year. This is done between the Commercial Manager and me. In this we really worry about maintaining the existing business, accepting that in volume terms 15% of our business potential is falling away every year.

You see, you have got to understand the way the parent company operates. Central funds will be made available for capital projects where one can demonstrate a market demand for a new business. But product innovation has got to be financed out of revenues.

We do have product development meetings . . . . usually twice a year at which the product range for a particular area is assessed and we decide whether we need to change course. These meetings include the marketing people. We usually have meetings every 3 months or so within the technical function to prepare for these meetings . . We have got to guide the marketing people!

For implementing product innovation

Technical Director:

Our experience tells us that one person must be made responsible for a particular project. It can take us up to 5 years to

develop a major electronic instrument. You
see, very often a development will grow in
scope as we go along. Fresh ideas come
along which are then incorporated. Often,
our customers for whom we are doing the
development work change their mind, which of
course drags out the whole process.

Laboratory Engineering Manager:

Development work here is carried out by the
technical function with assistance from
marketing . . . manufacturing becomes
involved later, particularly when a product
update is being undertaken.

We are working to develop a control manual
for product development, and at present we
do keep minutes, particularly for the
externally funded projects - look, here are
some for a NCB development, which we keep on
the computer . . . that's really because
they ask us to in order to note changes in
the development specification.

We monitor internally funded development
work every 6 months. In the case of
externally funded work, progress is
monitored monthly. No, the MD does not get
involved at all in the electronics
development work, but that's because he has
not been here long. The previous MD did not
take any interest in electronic
developments, because he was a components
man . . . they tend to poke their noses
into activities they know something about.

Unfortunately, new product developments not
infrequently need to be stopped so that we
can devote more effort to current cost-
cutting exercises. It's sad, but that's
life at the moment.

SCORING OF THE HIDDEN STRUCTURES

On the basis of the interview data collected
within Saline Instruments Ltd (relevant excerpts of
which have been reported above verbatim), the firm's
informal working structures were scored as in Tables
6.5 amd 6.6

The Less Innovative Firms

Table 6.5

SALINE STRUCTURES FOR INITIATING PRODUCT INNOVATION

1.1   Specialisation

(i)   Do ideas for possible new products stem predominantly from one department, or do several departments involve themselves intimately in this task? (Functional specialisation)

Low   ☒ One function only

☐ Marketing and R&D

High   ☐ Marketing, R&D and other(s)

(ii)   By what means do those suggesting ideas get their inspiration? Are any specific activities engaged in – like brainstorming sessions – to increase the potential number of ideas? (Role specialisation)

Low   ☒ Ad hoc

☐ Ad hoc and analytical techniques
            e.g. lost orders, exhibitions, market surveys

High   ☐ Ad hoc and analytical techniques, and regular and
            formal brainstorming, buzz sessions etc

1.2   Formalisation

(i)   To what extent are those who involve themselves in suggesting ideas for possible new products given guidance or guidelines on this task in writing? (Written guidance)

Low   ☒ Not at all

☐ To some extent

High   ☐ Extensively

(ii)   To what extent is information on ideas for possible new products exchanged in writing between those involved? (Written communication)

Low   ☐ Predominantly spoken

☐ More spoken than written

High   ☒ More written than spoken

136

SALINE STRUCTURES FOR INITIATING PRODUCT INNOVATION continued

1.3   Standardisation

(i)   What guidance is given on the sort of new product ideas the company is seeking? (Consistency in control)

    Low   ☐ Business mission delineated

              ☐ Product market area delineated

    High   ☒ Product area delineated

(ii)   How frequently are formal meetings held at which suggestions for possible new products are discussed? (Frequency of reviews)

    Low   ☐ Less frequently than every 3 months

              ☒ At between 1 month and 3 monthly intervals

    High   ☐ Monthly or more frequently

1.4   Centralisation

How much influence does the CEO exert over the flow of ideas for possible new products? (Power retention by CEO)

    Low   ☐ He encourages as many ideas to be put forward as possible - the more the merrier

              ☐ He encourages ideas within the confines of the delineated strategy

    High   ☒ He seeks to keep tight control over the sort of ideas which are put forward

1.5   Stratification

From what level in the organisation are ideas typically taken up? (Seniority of dominant coalition)

    Low   ☐ Departmental executive level

              ☒ H O D level

    High   ☐ Board level

The Less Innovative Firms

Table 6.6

SALINE STRUCTURES FOR IMPLEMENTING PRODUCT INNOVATION

2.1   Specialisation

(i)   Which department or departments are intimately involved in the development process? (Functional specialisation)

        Low   ☐ R&D

                    ☒ Marketing and R&D

        High   ☐ Marketing, R&D and other(s)

(ii)   Certain types of activities can be particularly important in the development process. Do you, for example, have persons who assume responsibility for the following roles? (Role specialisation)

(1)   Business/project management (i.e. product championship)
(2)   Entrepreneurial interpretation of market trends (market gatekeeping)
(3)   Analysis of scientific and engineering trends affecting the development (technical gatekeeping)
(4)   Manufacturing/quality gatekeeping
(5)   Godfathering (sponsorship by a senior member)

        Low   ☐ 2 or less roles are specifically provided for

                    ☒ 3-4 roles are specifically provided for

        High   ☐ All roles are specifically provided for

2.2   Formalisation

(i)   In what form are those involved in the development process given guidance or guidelines on their work? (Written guidance)

        Low   ☒ The process is explained verbally

                    ☐ Some written guidelines are given

        High   ☐ A control manual is provided

(ii)   In what way is progress on specific development tasks noted? (Written communication)

        Low   ☒ Informal notes are kept

                    ☐ Formal notes are issued as required

        High   ☐ Formal minutes of meetings are issued

138

SALINE STRUCTURES FOR IMPLEMENTING PRODUCT INNOVATION continued

2.3   Standardisation

(i)   Are the same development criteria applied to control each project? For example, has each project an equal chance of being stopped? (Consistency in control)

Low   ☐ Totally different criteria

              ☒ Somewhat different criteria

High   ☐ Essentially similar criteria

(ii)   How frequently is progress on development work monitored formally? (Frequency of reviews)

Low   ☐ Less frequently than every 3 months

              ☒ At between 1 month and 3 monthly intervals

High   ☐ Monthly or more frequently

2.4   Centralisation

What control or influence does the CEO exert over the development work? (Power retention by CEO)

Low   ☐ He expects others to get on with it independently

              ☒ He is kept in touch with progress

High   ☐ He is informed of progress in detail

2.5   Stratification

At what level is responsibility for the overall success of a project development assumed i.e. at whom is the finger pointed if something goes wrong? (Seniority of dominant coalition)

Low   ☐ Department executive level

              ☒ H O D level

High   ☐ Board level

The Less Innovative Firms

SUMMARY

This case illustrates product innovation in a typical technology-driven firm in which new products are suggested by technical personnel, most often on the basis of requests from dominant customers. At no stage in the product innovation procedure are marketing personnel involved in a serious way. In fact, in this firm marketing has not been formally recognised as an essential operating function - the commercial function is merely looked to for the purpose of selling products once these are established on the range.

There is little or no communication between the technical function and persons nominally representing the marketing function. This is not helped by the fact that nearly all technical personnel go to lunch at 12.00 noon, whilst commercial personnel traditionally lunch at 1 pm in the same dining room after the technical people have left. There is little respect for the technical abilities of commercial people on the part of technical people. In fact, to have joined the commercial function in this firm is taken as an indication that a person has turned his or her back on keeping abreast of technological developments.

BATTALION MANUFACTURING COMPANY LTD

This case is of interest because it illustrates the real dangers accompanying lack of attention to product innovation in firms which now find themselves operating in a far more turbulent technological environment. The exposition followed in this case differs somewhat from the pattern of the previous studies for reasons which are readily apparent. It was the only firm visited during the research where only one person was interviewed - in this case the Managing Director - who was frank in his comments.

BACKGROUND

The firm was established during the First World War and incorporated as a limited liability company in 1930. The present Chairman and major shareholder is the son of the founder. To this day the firm remains privately owned. Until early 1981 there were three manufacturing sites in the UK, but in April 1981 two sites were closed in order to reduce overheads with the loss of 140 jobs. The total number of employees of the firm in mid-1981 was 240. In the words of the Managing Director:

> We have been hit by competition and the recession and the strength of the pound - quite a lot of adverse factors in the last 2 or 3 years. And ours is a very labour intensive industry, so as soon as one starts to cut back on output, then numbers employed fall dramatically. We have cut back a lot recently. At one time we needed all three factories for reasons of production flexibility, particularly when demand was high, to avert disruptions caused by strikes. But, of course, labour problems are now not what they used to be. Also, our products have become smaller in size, so we now have the floor space at this site to make all we can sell.

The Less Innovative Firms

The company makes and markets electrical
indicating instruments - ammeters, voltmeters,
frequency meters and accessories for these. The
products are marketed in various different case
styles. The MD:

> We don't get into the more complicated
> instruments. We are, what I would say, at
> the bottom end of the market.

Asked what factors were mainly responsible for
the present difficult trading conditions, the MD
replied:

> The market has been affected by the
> recession, but I would not say that there is
> an overall decline in it worldwide . . . . .
> The fact that digital instruments have come
> on the scene has not really affected our
> sector of the market as much as the test
> side. But there is a lot more competition
> than before. For example, products have
> tended to become more standardised,
> particularly for case dimensions and the way
> movements are made. Consequently, all sorts
> of people are able to put them together who
> could not previously . . . . particularly
> people in countries which have much lower
> labour costs than ourselves.

> We have been affected by competition from
> really all over the world - Japan, Far
> Eastern countries and especially Italy and
> Spain, which are able to produce traditional
> instruments at lower costs than we can. In
> the case of the Japanese it is higher
> productivity which keeps their costs down -
> they will not, for example, look at the more
> specialist type of instrument which we do,
> because the quantities are not there.
> However, as far as movements are concerned
> the Japanese excel in large quantities made
> well and cheaply. An example is the market
> for level indicators for tape recorders,
> where there are vast quantities involved,
> and nobody can get anywhere near the
> Japanese. Sometimes they don't make

142

all their products in Japan, but they are
designed there, and the production is
organised from there.

We have also been hit by European
competition and really it's more difficult
to understand why they are able to produce
cheaper than us . . . I think to some
extent the reason is productivity . . . and
the rate of exchange has hit us too . . .
but it is more difficult to put your finger
on the fundamental reasons. Generally
speaking, I think there are a lot more
people producing our type of product than
there ever were 10 years ago. So one is
bound to be affected. .

Asked about the role of marketing, the MD said:

Yes, well, um: I take responsibility for
all sales and marketing. We don't have a
sales manager or a sales director or
marketing. We have several people on the
sales side, but not at the level you are
talking about. We have a UK sales
representative and he reports to me . . .
In our particular sector of the industry the
sales and marketing side has not been too
important, because, until 3 or 4 years ago
the problem was not selling or marketing the
product, but one of making enough to satisfy
demand. Consequently, we haven't got the
sales and marketing set-up that we would
like to have now.

Researcher:

The feeling I get with companies in the
situation you have described is that until
about 3 years ago you were making healthy
amounts of money because you could sell
everything you were making. Now competition
has come along and it would be surprising if
margins were not squeezed and things were
not somewhat different.

MD:

Yes, absolutely. In fact it's no real

secret that we are operating in a break-even situation at the present time. We made a loss last year, but that was perhaps a paper loss because we did a number of things designed to strengthen the future of the company. [They bought another company].

Researcher:

Presumably there have been ups and downs in your industry before. Is this just one of the troughs?

MD:

I have not seen a situation before as bad as it is at the present time. I believe we can compete as a company with any of the UK manufacturers in our line of products. Where the problem is, is in competing with the overseas competition . . . When I say compete I am really talking about price. Technically, there are no problems. So much at the present time and in the future is going to depend on price.

Researcher:

Do you think, with hindsight, that had you had someone here keeping an eye on what was happening in Europe on what are now very awkward competitors, you might have been able to avoid the break-even situation in which you now find yourself?

MD:

I am sure we could. The problem is partly caused by standards and here we can criticise ourselves, or SIMA (the trade association) or the BSI or whatever. In the end it comes back to British manufacturers in as much as we are not well organised among ourselves. We have not developed a common technical standard, as far as the products we're in are concerned. The DIN standard has not been adopted because the

Germans were that much further ahead with
their standardisation efforts.

If we (British manufacturers) had realised
what was being done, and that
standardisation was moving the way it was,
we could also have brought out our own
standard, which could have been adopted as
a European standard, just as the DIN
standard is now. What happened was that
the Germans were so far ahead with standardisation that their standards have been
adopted. And, because German manufacturers
have been several steps ahead of us, we
have got some catching up to do in terms of
producing to their standard.

Asked about the importance of new products
within his company's recent marketing strategy, the
MD replied:

I don't think our new products are really so
much new products as modifications of
standard products. I am really talking
about specialised applications of dial work
or accessories or whatever. They are not
really revolutionary products in themselves.
I think, however, that they are important,
in that there is always a market for
specialist things whatever they are. But I
think a company like ours cannot survive
without standard products, and so it is very
important for us to compete with a standard
range . . . and I come back to this . . .
the specials are, if you like, the 'jam on
it', but it's very important that one does
the standard work as well.

Researcher:

Could you foresee that situation ever
changing in your company? I am asking the
question to get a feel for the importance
you attach to developing new products.

MD:

I think, and this is quite new thinking on
our part, that we as a company need to find

a new product of some sort - not
necessarily the same thing which we have
been used to making. In fact, we are
actively looking for something that can use
the skills which we have within our
company, to broaden our base a bit from
what we have done in the past. We don't
just want to make more instruments of
different types, but something perhaps
which is different. It need not be an
instrument, but we've obviously got to use
the skills we have developed over the
years.

We have been actively looking, over the
last 6 months, for something that does just
that. But more than that I can't say . . .

. . Yes, recently we have bought a little
company which was an old-established company. We bought their transformer set-up
and that has gone very well indeed; and we
are very pleased with that. And it may
well be that there are opportunities for us
with transformers more generally than we
are doing at the moment. The way we have
approached the opportunity is to sell
transformers as accessories for the
instruments to people we already do
business with. This has, I suppose, opened
our eyes to opportunities which could be
viable with our existing customer base.

Asked whether he could give an example of a
recent new product development, the MD replied:

Our new products are not completely new
products. They are improvements to existing
products; changes in case style - the new
square DIN range is the best example. And
we also make updates to the movements
themselves, which does not affect the look
of the instrument. Bear in mind, we are
still selling some products which were
designed in the 1930s and 1940s.

THE FORMAL STRUCTURE

As is normal practice in many smaller family-owned British firms, the Managing Director has been given overall responsibility for day-to-day operations. The executive control structure is shown in Table 6.7. The Technical Director has been with the firm for many years, the Works Director joined recently, as is explained below.

Table 6.7

BATTALION - EXECUTIVE CONTROL STRUCTURE

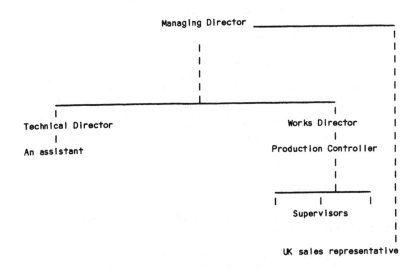

THE HIDDEN STRUCTURES

For initiating product innovation

Asked who typically suggests ideas for possible new products (really product updates) the MD replied:

> Generally myself, or we have one UK
> representative and a couple of agents. They
> would make comments to me about things, and
> I will then take them up with the Technical
> Director. They always come through me.

Asked whether he ever called people together to
discuss specific opportunities for new products, the
MD replied:

> We are just doing this now. In fact, we
> have decided to do it with respect to one
> particular product - it's a cheap product we
> make for the battery charger industry. We
> are doing this in conjunction with PERA to
> bring out a completely new design. I think
> one of the problems in this industry is that
> it is very specialised, and occasionally
> someone from outside the industry looking in
> can provide useful insight.

> In effect, PERA are acting as consultants to
> us. It's the first time we have used them
> in this sense. We first involved them in a
> value-engineering exercise, but now their
> involvement has grown. Initially, it was
> just a cost-cutting exercise, but when we
> decided we needed to do a complete overhaul
> of an existing product, we decided to use
> PERA as someone who is not really in the
> trade to bounce ideas off. This has been
> extremely useful to us.

Reflecting on the way ideas for new products are
generated in his firm, the MD said:

> Our problem is that we have changed from a
> situation where we could pick and choose
> what we made - the problem was one of making
> it, rather than selling it - to one in which
> we find ourselves with a certain amount of
> catching up to do. Now it really is a case
> of looking around [outside the firm] and it
> tends to be me who does it.

For evaluating alternatives

Commenting on the way new product opportunities are
assessed, the MD replied:

148

We tend to look at updates of our products together as a Board and decide that we must improve or change a design and so allocate whatever money is required for the purpose. . . We look at capital expenditure projects on a year-to-year basis and we do what we think we can afford. We do not tend to set aside a certain amount of money every year for R & D.

One of the problems which we face at the moment is that we do not have enough development time available. . . Faced with the situation of very reduced margins, as we are at the moment, I find it a hard decision to put money into areas where you are necessarily uncertain of the returns. So we have tended to stick with what we've got. This is particularly so in a small company in which one tends to deal with the problems of the moment. Until recent years these were getting the stuff out of the factory gate; now they are saving cash.

Furthermore, three years ago we had a union coming here which we never had before. We had a Works Director who instantly retired - all these sorts of problems took precedence over the sort we have just been talking about.

For implementing product innovation

The MD commented as follows:

We are now having regular formal meetings to progress the battery charger indicator development. We are meeting at the moment at intervals of between 2 weeks and a month. The intention was to meet every 2 or 3 weeks, but the holidays have interfered with this. The meetings involve the Works Director and the PERA representative, in addition to myself and the Technical Director. I am really wearing the marketing hat. What we are doing is having regular meetings, with each of us agreeing what we are to do before the next meeting.

Asked whether he could foresee a time, after the
present emergency, when he would delegate the
development of new products, the MD replied:

> I don't think I would delegate the task
> completely, no. What I would like to see in
> this company is more delegation of sales and
> marketing matters. I would like a sales
> manager and I would like more time spent on
> development work. It's not the appropriate
> time to do it at the moment. The
> concentrated effort at the moment is on
> surviving, because we are operating on a
> shoestring, as many other companies are.
> But the present problems have brought it
> home to me that we haven't done enough on
> product development in the past. We must
> certainly do more of that. We must
> certainly also do far more on the marketing
> side than we have ever done previously. In
> a way it takes a recession for you to really
> analyse what you are doing and to analyse
> the changed position of the company. . .
>
> I tend to be in a situation at the moment
> where I am responsible for everything.
> That's got to change, we can't go on in the
> present way for ever and a day . . and, as
> I've said, we are very much operating on a
> shoestring. So for the future, we have got
> to develop new products. It's no good us
> sitting back - our products really haven't
> changed that much in 60 years. We have got
> to develop something completely new. We
> are all aware of this, but I think,
> truthfully, we have only actively been
> looking for something really new in the last
> 12 months. Previous to that one could never
> say that we have actively looked and pursued
> any ideas for new products. If one came up,
> it was good; well, we accepted it, but if it
> didn't work, it didn't really matter all
> that much, because we were making an ad-
> equate return on the capital employed. So
> there was never any real effort needed for
> new products . . . Yes, we are very self-
> critical at the moment, that's why I am
> happy to talk with you and perhaps tell you
> things which I shouldn't. But I'm quite

happy to talk to anybody at the moment on this subject . . .

Asked what sort of companies he admires, and would like to model his own on in the future, the MD replied:

> I admire certain French companies making similar products to our own. Although they are basically similar instrument manufacturers they are doing all sorts of things - like test sets, multimeters, which we don't get into. It does seem to me that they have put a lot more effort into new product development than we have. You only have to look at their catalogues to see the range of things they are able to do, when on the face of it they are companies of a similar size to us. They have somehow managed to put the effort and emphasis on a wider product base than we have. I would be very interested to know how much money companies of that size and type spend on R&D and what proportion of products they factor.

SCORING OF THE HIDDEN STRUCTURES

On the basis of the interview data collected within Battalion Instruments Ltd (relevant excerpts of which have been reported above verbatim), the firm's informal working structures were scored as in Tables 6.8 and 6.9.

The Less Innovative Firms

Table 6.8

BATTALION STRUCTURES FOR INITIATING PRODUCT INNOVATION

1.1   Specialisation

(i)   Do ideas for possible new products stem predominantly from one department, or do several departments involve themselves intimately in this task? (Functional specialisation)

        Low   ☒ One function only

                      ☐ Marketing and R&D

        High   ☐ Marketing, R&D and other(s)

(ii)   By what means do those suggesting ideas get their inspiration? Are any specific activities engaged in - like brainstorming sessions - to increase the potential number of ideas? (Role specialisation)

        Low   ☒ Ad hoc

                      ☐ Ad hoc and analytical techniques
                           e.g. lost orders, exhibitions, market surveys

        High   ☐ Ad hoc and analytical techniques, and regular and
                           formal brainstorming, buzz sessions etc

1.2   Formalisation

(i)   To what extent are those who involve themselves in suggesting ideas for possible new products given guidance or guidelines on this task in writing? (Written guidance)

        Low   ☒ Not at all

                      ☐ To some extent

        High   ☐ Extensively

(ii) To what extent is information on ideas for possible new products exchanged in writing between those involved? (Written communication)

        Low   ☐ Predominantly spoken

                      ☐ More spoken than written

        High   ☒ More written than spoken

BATTALION STRUCTURES FOR INITIATING PRODUCT INNOVATION continued

1.3   Standardisation

(i)   What guidance is given on the sort of new product ideas the company is seeking? (Consistency in control)

     Low   ☐ Business mission delineated

              ☐ Product market area delineated

     High   ☒ Product area delineated

(ii) How frequently are formal meetings held at which suggestions for possible new products are discussed? (Frequency of reviews)

     Low   ☐ Less frequently than every 3 months

              ☒ At between 1 month and 3 monthly intervals

     High   ☐ Monthly or more frequently

1.4   Centralisation

How much influence does the CEO exert over the flow of ideas for possible new products? (Power retention by CEO)

     Low   ☐ He encourages as many ideas to be put forward as possible - the more the merrier

              ☐ He encourages ideas within the confines of the delineated strategy

     High   ☒ He seeks to keep tight control over the sort of ideas which are put forward

1.5   Stratification

From what level in the organisation are ideas typically taken up? (Seniority of dominant coalition)

     Low   ☐ Departmental executive level

              ☒ H O D level

     High   ☐ Board level

The Less Innovative Firms

Table 6.9

BATTALION STRUCTURES FOR IMPLEMENTING PRODUCT INNOVATION

2.1   Specialisation

(i)   Which department or departments are intimately involved in the development process? (Functional specialisation)

        Low   ☐   R&D

                   ☒   Marketing and R&D

        High   ☐   Marketing, R&D and other(s)

(ii)   Certain types of activities can be particularly important in the development process.   Do you, for example, have persons who assume responsibility for the following roles? (Role specialisation)

(1)   Business/project management (i.e. product championship)
(2)   Entrepreneurial interpretation of market trends (market gatekeeping)
(3)   Analysis of scientific and engineering trends affecting the development (technical gatekeeping)
(4)   Manufacturing/quality gatekeeping
(5)   Godfathering (sponsorship by a senior member)

        Low   ☐   2 or less roles are specifically provided for

                   ☒   3-4 roles are specifically provided for

        High   ☐   All roles are specifically provided for

2.2   Formalisation

(i)   In what form are those involved in the development process given guidance or guidelines on their work? (Written guidance)

        Low   ☒   The process is explained verbally

                   ☐   Some written guidelines are given

        High   ☐   A control manual is provided

(ii)   In what way is progress on specific development tasks noted? (Written communication)

        Low   ☒   Informal notes are kept

                   ☐   Formal notes are issued as required

        High   ☐   Formal minutes of meetings are issued

154

BATTALION STRUCTURES FOR IMPLEMENTING PRODUCT INNOVATION continued

2.3 Standardisation

(i) Are the same development criteria applied to control each project? For example, has each project an equal chance of being stopped? (Consistency in control)

Low   ☐   Totally different criteria

                ☒   Somewhat different criteria

High   ☐   Essentially similar criteria

(ii) How frequently is progress on development work monitored formally? (Frequency of reviews)

Low   ☐   Less frequently than every 3 months

                ☒   At between 1 month and 3 monthly intervals

High   ☐   Monthly or more frequently

2.4 Centralisation

What control or influence does the CEO exert over the development work? (Power retention by CEO)

Low   ☐   He expects others to get on with it independently

                ☒   He is kept in touch with progress

High   ☐   He is informed of progress in detail

2.5 Stratification

At what level is responsibility for the overall success of a project development assumed i.e. at whom is the finger pointed if something goes wrong? (Seniority of dominant coalition)

Low   ☐   Department executive level

                ☒   H O D level

High   ☐   Board level

The Less Innovative Firms

SUMMARY

The desperate situation this firm finds itself in as a consequence of inadequate attention to product innovation has been described vividly by the Managing Director. There are many firms which have in the past operated in a production-orientated way. Only a few of these have managed to survive the recession. The case serves as a warning to all firms, especially smaller firms, which although once leaders in product innovation, have allowed their technological lead to be eroded.

Chapter Seven

CURRENT TRENDS IN STRUCTURING

This chapter considers the main operational
issues arising out of the case investigations and
also comments on current developments in
organisational structuring aimed at efficient and
effective product innovation in manufacturing firms.
The first part of the chapter concerns itself with
why more and more firms are having to adopt speedy
product innovation as a competitive weapon and why
this strategy frequently requires a considerably
increased commitment to R&D expenditures. The
second, more important part of the chapter,
discusses current trends in organising for speedy
and efficient product innovation.
Lorenz (1984) and Business Week (1984) have
provided several dramatic examples of well-known
firms which are currently speeding the time taken to
develop new products. For example, IBM is reported
as having beaten the personal computer industry's 24
month development norm by almost 10 months.
Similarly, General Motors, Ford, Volkswagen and many
other mass-producers of cars, which have typically
taken 4-7 years to develop a new model, are now
attempting to get nearer the 3 years it typically
takes a Japanese car manufacturer. Procter and
Gamble is reported as recently having halved the
development time on many of its packaged products
from 2 years to 1 year. Xerox, too, is reported as
having halved the time and resources needed to bring
many new products to market.

---

* The latter part of this chapter is based on the article : Johne, F.A.
(1984), How experienced product innovators organize. Journal of Product
Innovation Management, 1,4 (December) : 210-223.

Whilst it is extremely difficult to compare average development times across firms because of differences in the levels of sophistication of the products being developed, there can be little doubt that the active product innovators described in Chapter 5 have learned a great deal about this aspect in particular. Underlying the trend towards quicker development times are, of course, technological and marketing factors. On the technological front it was seen that the effect of electronics has been particularly strong. This is because electronic control configurations can now be easily changed, especially with the aid of CAD, which has led to an acceleration in the development of new generations of products. Whereas in the past product generations used to change approximately every 10 years, such change now occurs every 2 or 3 years, whenever there is an appreciable electronic content to the product.

On the marketing front, competition is being waged by an increasing number of firms in world markets rather than in purely national or local markets. A direct consequence of this is greater pressure on all firms to offer customers something new unless they want to risk loosing business to competitors. In addition, there is a tendency on the part of many firms to use shorter life cycles as a marketing weapon. Not only is this a means for eliminating competitors from particular markets, but it can also be a most profitable strategy for reaping super-normal profits. Indeed, in many high technology product markets, it is frequently claimed that being 1 year quicker to market can double a firms's sales revenue from a new product. After all, it is a well-known phenomenon that early entrants can often charge a premium price, particularly in those high technology markets where customers are prepared to pay higher prices for products which give them a technological lead over their own competitors.

It is clear that the amounts spent by firms on R&D vary considerably. Whilst spending large amounts of money in this way will not ensure entry to high technology markets, it is nonetheless a necessary condition for gaining entry. And there can be no doubt that it is these markets which are currently experiencing the highest rate of expansion. For example, the Economist (1984) in an article entitled "Low-tech engineers get ready to meet their receivers" suggests that there are far greater business opportunities in meeting the demands of high technology markets, such as electrical and electronic engineering than there are in meeting the demands of lower technology markets, such as mechanical engineering. Hence, it argues, firms are far more likely to survive the present recession by aiming to supply growing market segments.

As was discussed in Chapter 4 and shown in Table 4.1, active corporate product innovation requires considerable investment in terms of R&D expenditures. In terms of aggregate national R&D spending the US remains the world leader with expenditures more than double the combined totals of Europe and Japan (Business Week 1984a). In terms of absolute amounts spent by firms, General Motors, IBM, AT & T and Ford are by far the most active, each spending on average over $2,000,000,000 on R&D. Percentage of sales figures provide even greater insight, particularly across industries. Whilst some firms spend little or nothing on R&D (as was seen in Chapter 6), several active product innovator firms in computer related industries currently spend over 15% of sales revenue on R&D, with a small number spending over $15,000 per employee in the US.

The issue facing British firms to-day has been well-expressed in a recent survey of current marketing practice and performance in the UK. In the survey Hooley et al. (1984) found a predominance of markets deemed by their respondents to be in maturity or decline, which led them to suggest the following strategic imperatives:

> First, it would seem that an essential prerequisite for corporate success in complex and turbulent markets is a high level of flexibility and adaptability in an organisation's systems, attitudes and structures. There is an over-riding need to avoid over-dependence on a too narrow or rigid trading base. Secondly, the constant shifts in the relative value of products and markets necessitates the setting of clear priorities in resource allocation. Thirdly, organisation structures must be designed which can accommodate strategic flexibility. Strategy can only be successfully implemented if

an appropriate structure exists in the organisation. ....Flexibility and adaptability are not simply related to attitudes and systems; they are a function of organisational design.

Behind Hooley's imperatives lies the assumption that firms have control over their own destiny, which may well not be the case. For example, sometimes firms are required to fulfil the functions asked of them within a larger portfolio of businesses or SBUs. In such circumstances the top management of a SBU may not be permitted to rejuvenate their own business unit through active product innovation policies. This phenomenon has been referred to as the principal fallacy of the portfolio concept by Pascale & Athos (1982:40) who argue:

......all that frequently stands between a division being viewed as a cash cow or a star is management's creativity in seeing how to reposition their products in tune with the marketplace. [The Japanese firm] Matsushita gives the divisions a major responsibility for doing that - and spurs them on with a lot of additional help and pressure from the product group specialists.

When firms do have freedom to act in their own best interests the structures discussed in Chapter 2 and the examples given in Chapter 5 will be found useful for finding ways in which product innovation can be pursued most cost-effectively. The finding that active and experienced product innovators have learned to use predominantly loose structures for initiation and predominantly tight structures for implementation are certainly interesting and intuitively appealing, particularly because they accord with assertions made in the analytical literature on innovation. But for the purpose of pinpointing implications of direct use to management involved actively in product innovation it is now necessary to consider carefully the various sub-activities embraced within each of the two main phases of initiation and implementation.

Taking first the phase of <u>implementation</u>, which covers product development proper, test marketing and launching, the case investigations in Chapter 5 show that active and experienced product innovator firms attach great importance to adhering to formal control mechanisms. In this way progress can be checked and coordinated to ensure efficient development. In the wider study reported in Chapter 4, four of the eight active product innovator firms studied possessed a control manual for coordinating the sub-activities involved in implementing. The remaining four firms all used various types of check lists for controlling and coordinating separate implementation sub-activities.

Hence, as far as product development proper, test marketing and launching is concerned, the wider findings lend support to Booz Allen & Hamilton's (1982) assertion that there is now far more formality in the new product development process in successful firms. Our findings do, however, conflict with those of Feldman & Page (1984) who state: "In the nine companies we observed there did not seem to be much order in the process. Few had documents spelling out the procedure, and if they had them, they were more often honored in the breach". One possible explanation for the conflict is that Feldman & Page's sample included a large number of firms which were not market leaders and which therefore may not be experienced in product innovation procedures. Certainly, all the evidence provided in case investigations of active and experienced product innovator firms suggests that such firms have taken considerable trouble to streamline and closely control the sub-activities involved in implementing product innovation.

The main implication of the wider findings for management is that firms with little or no experience of product innovation stand to benefit considerably by more tightly organising implementation tasks, not only for the purpose of reducing development costs, but also to shorten the time needed to get new products to market successfully. This is likely to involve such firms in making changes to the levels of specialisation, formalisation and standardisation. Centralisation is likely to be already high in less active product innovator firms, but important changes will almost certainly need to be made in terms of stratification - particularly in ascribing ultimate responsibility for implementation to top officers.

The managerial implications of the results for

initiating product development, i.e. generating new ideas, screening and testing and developing ideas in concept are somewhat different from what had been anticipated. It will have been noticed that the findings concerning structural configurations are focussed predominantly on how ideas for possible new products are generated. While in general terms looser structures are undoubtedly functional for this purpose, case examples of recent product innovations revealed that active and experienced product innovator firms temper looseness during initiation very carefully, as is explained below.

The generation of new ideas is generally not a problem in active product innovator firms. Such firms are typically staffed with large numbers of bright, well-qualified persons who are well able to suggest how existing products might be improved on technological grounds and on how the latest advances in technology can be used to develop completely new products. A much more important problem in active product innovator firms is how the creativity of well-qualified staff can be channelled so that ideas are suggested which fit in with a particular new product strategy. The issue was well expressed by one senior manager in the following words: "I don't want ideas on better toasters. I am sure we could make a super toaster, but we're not in that business. We're competing in a particular segment of the stand-alone instrument market - so it's better or completely new ways of meeting the test and measurement requirements of chosen customers that I am looking for".

It is relevant to note here that in a recent broadly-based study Booz Allen & Hamilton (1982) found that a mere 7 ideas are now required, on average, to generate one successful new product. This led them to state: "Ideas generated today are more clearly defined and better focussed than they were 5 to 10 years ago". From the results of our own study we would suggest that there is another reason why fewer ideas appear to be needed now, which is connected with the way such ideas are tested more rigorously in concept in many firms. Rockwell & Particelli (1980) of Booz Allen & Hamilton have, in a separate publication, referred to this activity as "up-front analysis", during which ideas for new products are subjected to extensive and oftentimes expensive preliminary appraisal. Specifically, we suspect that the increased scrutiny given "up-front" to ideas for possible new products is responsible in many firms for far greater care being exercised over the quality of suggestions being made. That is to say, the emphasis during initiation is swinging away in many firms from sheer quantity of creative inputs to increased emphasis on meeting strategic market targets qualitatively.

We regard the increased emphasis given to "up-front analysis" in many firms as a particularly important refinement of product innovation initiation procedures. Indeed, in several experienced product innovator firms the potential return of spending quite large sums of money on concept testing and development was stressed. One R&D manager expressed it as follows: "At the concept stage we are testing the new product idea. It's worth spending up to $100,000 on this - sometimes it's even more. The downside risk to the company is far less than letting the market test a fully developed new product costing say $5 million. And, even if the project is a flop, we will have learned something for next time".

In all active product innovator firms great importance was placed on "up-front analysis". In several firms up to $100,000 will be made available for developing and testing a new product idea in concept under the leadership of a project engineer. This expenditure is committed expressly for the purpose of exploring the new product idea further before making a decision on whether or not to engage in full-scale development work. Indeed, so clear is the divide between initiation and implementation that it is accepted practice in many active product innovator firms for a celebration to be held at the end of the initiation phase. Then, irrespective of whether an exploratory project is allocated further money for full-scale development or whether it is "killed" for either technical and/or commercial reasons, a drinks party is held.

Case investigations of product developments in less active product innovator firms indicated no clear divide between initiation phase expenditures and implementation phase expenditures. Indeed, there appears to be an implicit acceptance that all expenditure ought to be justified in terms of final commercial success. Consequently, once a new product idea has been approved, a project often gains a momentum of its own which is only capable of being stopped by market forces after launch.

The main implication of these findings for management with respect to initiation activities is that firms with little or no experience of product innovation stand to benefit by separating initiation-related tasks from implementation-related tasks. There can be no doubt that technological product innovation is expensive and that it also requires leaps of faith on the part of top management in response to ideas put forward by often quite junior members of staff. As a safeguard against expensive and embarrassing mistakes it would appear to be particularly advantageous to explore in concept as many new product ideas as the resources of the firm will allow. To do so requires members of staff to be released from on-going operational tasks and to be given freedom in exploring and developing their ideas in depth. For this purpose a certain loosening in control and coordination is called for, along the lines practised by active and experienced product innovator firms, as was described in Chapter 5.

Chapter Eight

CONCLUSION

Several writers have stressed that much decision taking in business fails to follow normative textbook models (Feldman & Page, 1984; Mintzberg et al. 1976; Verhage et al. 1981). The research reported in this book has identified a sample of active and experienced product innovator firms which have taken positive steps to follow certain procedures in a near-textbook manner. The fact that most firms in an industry do not adhere to best current organisational practice is not really surprising. What is exciting and challenging is that a relatively small number of firms in one industry, in which product innovation is of great importance for competitive reasons, is pursuing organisational practices which have been shown to be functional for getting new technically advanced products to market efficiently.

Considerable problems do, of course, arise over the measurement of efficiency in product innovation. It can be measured in two main ways depending on whether an individual product or the firm as a whole is the focus of study. Individual product success is a limited measure because most firms can achieve it if they take low market-related and low technology-related risks. A better measure is success in terms of impact on total company sales, and also in terms of ultimate profit contribution. To achieve these corporate objectives in an industry afflicted by complex and turbulent changes in technology requires a firm to add new technically advanced products on to its product range quickly and successfully. It is by using appropriate organisational mechanisms that this activity can be expedited.

Conclusion

The actual organisational mechanisms which have
been considered in this book are those which
facilitate tactical or operational decisions. It
was shown that while there are clear differences in
the formal mechanisms used by active product
innovator firms compared with those used by less
active product innovator firms, it is informal
structures which reveal the most important
differences in modes of operation. It was seen in
the case investigations in Chapters 5 and 6 that
active product innovator firms combine successfully
the dual activities of market pull and technological
push through carefully selecting an appropriate
customer base.

What the case investigations in this book have
revealed is that active and experienced product
innovator firms in the instrument manufacturing
industry have learned to handle product innovation
tasks as part of their on-going business activities.
On the other hand, less active product innovator
firms frequently find it necessary to develop new
products as a separate activity, which means that
the core business is not exposed regularly to
outside influences. This is an important finding
because corporate rejuvenation requires an
organisation to interact positively with changes in
its environment and this is clearly more difficult
if the core business is sheltered from such changes.

Last, but not least, it must be stressed that
the case examples of product innovation practices in
active and experienced product innovator firms show
that there is no one right way to organise. However, what the analysis of informal or hidden structures discussed in this book has revealed is that
the organisational mechanisms used by active product
innovator firms do have a common underlying theme,
which is worthy of consideration by all firms which
want to streamline their development procedures.

BIBLIOGRAPHY AND REFERENCES

Ansoff, H.I. (1965), Corporate Strategy. Harmondsworth, Middlesex: Penguin.

Ansoff, H.I. et al. (1976), From strategic planning to strategic management, in Ansoff, H.I., R.P. Declerk and R.L. Hayes (eds.). From Strategic Planning to Strategic Management. London: John Wiley: 39-78.

Ansoff, H.I. (1984), Implanting Strategic Management. Englewood Cliffs, N.J.: Prentice Hall.

Baker, M.J. (1975), Marketing New Industrial Products. London: Macmillan.

Baldridge, J.V. & R.A. Burnham (1975), Organizational innovation: individual organizational and environmental factors. Administrative Science Quarterly, 20 (June): 165-176.

Benson, G. & J. Chasin (1976), The Structure of New Product Organization. New York: Amacom.

Booz, Allen & Hamilton (1982), New Products Management for the 1980s. New York: Booz, Allen & Hamilton Inc.

Burns, T. & G.M. Stalker (1961), The Management of Innovation. London: Tavistock Publications.

Business Week (1984), How Xerox speeds up the birth of new products. March 19: 42-43.

Business Week (1984a), A deepening commitment to R&D. July 9: 62.

Child, J. (1984), Organization: a guide to problems and practice. London: Harper & Row.

Choffray, J,M. and G.L. Lilien (1980), Industrial market segmentation by the structure of the purchasing process. Industrial Marketing Management, 9: 331-342.

Cooper, R.G. (1982), New product success in industrial firms. Industrial Marketing Management, 11: 215-223.

Cooper, R.G. (1983), The impact of new product strategies. Industrial Marketing Management, 12: 243-256.

Cooper, R.G. (1983a), The new product process: an empirically-based classification scheme. R&D Management, 13,1: 1-13.

Cooper, R.G. (1983b), A process model for industrial new product development. IEEE Transactions in Engineering Management, EM-30, 1 (February): 2-11.

Crawford, C.M. (1979), New product failure rates - facts and fallacies. Research Management, (Sept): 9-13.

Cummings, L.L. & M.J. O'Connell (1978), Organizational innovation: a model and needed research. Journal of Business Research, 6 (Jan): 33-50.

Dewar, R.D. & R.B. Duncan (1977), Implications for organizational design of structural alteration as a consequence of growth and innovation. Organization & Administrative Sciences, 8 (Summer-Fall): 203-222.

Dougherty, D.M., D.B. Stephens and D.E. Ezell (1984), The lasting qualities of PERT: preferences and perceptions of R&D project managers. R&D Management. 14,1: 47-56.

Doyle, P. (1979), Management structures and marketing strategies in UK industry. European Journal of Marketing, 13,5: 319-331.

Drucker, P.F. (1974), Management: Tasks, Responsibilities, Practices. New York: Harper Row.

Dunn, D.T. (1977), The rise and fall of ten venture groups. Business Horizons, (Oct.): 32-41.

Economist (1983), The new entrepreneurs: today's innovators are the same - only different. December 24: 59-71.

Economist (1984), Low-tech engineers get ready to meet their receivers. September 15: 73-74.

Fast, N.D. (1978), New venture departments: organizing for innovation. Industrial Marketing Management, 7: 77-88.

Fast, N.D. (1979), The future of industrial new venture departments. Industrial Marketing Management, 8: 264-273.

Feldman, L.P. & A.L. Page (1984), Principles versus practice in new product planning. The Journal of Product Innovation Management, 1,1: 43-55.

Freeman, C. (1974), The Economics of Industrial Innovation. Harmondsworth, Middlesex: Penguin.

Galbraith, J.R. and D.A. Nathanson (1979), The role of organization structure and the process of strategy implementation, in D.E. Schendel and C.W. Hofer (eds.), Strategic Management: A new view of Business Policy and Planning. Boston: Little Brown: 249-302.

Hage, J. & M. Aiken (1970). Social Change in Complex Organizations. New York: Random House.

Hill, R.M. and J.D. Hlavacek (1977), Learning from failure: ten guidelines for venture management. California Management Review, (Summer) XIX,4: 5-16.

Bibliography and References

Hippel von E. (1978), Successful industrial products from customer ideas. Journal of Marketing, (Jan.): 39-49.

Hippel von E. (1982), Get new products from customers. Harvard Business Review (March-April): 117-112.

Hopkins, D.S. (1974), Options in New-Product Organization. New York: The Conference Board.

Hopkins, D.S. (1975), The roles of project teams and venture groups in new product development. Research Management, 8 (Jan): 7-12.

Hopkins, D.S. (1981), New product winners and losers. R&D Management, (May): 12-17.

Hooley, G., C.J. West and J.E. Lynch (1984), Marketing in the UK: A Survey of Current Practice and Performance. Cookham: Institute of Marketing.

Johne, F.A. (1984), How experienced product innovators organize. Journal of Product Innovation Management, 1,4 (December): 210-223.

King, S. (1973), Developing New Brands. London: Pitman.

Kolodny, H.F. (1979), Evolution to a matrix organization. Academy of Management Review, 4,4: 543-553.

Lawrence, P.R. and J.W. Lorsch (1967), Organization and Environment: Managing Differentiation and Integration. Boston: Division of Research, Harvard Graduate School of Business Administration.

Lorenz, C. (1984), New product development: a vicious race to get ahead. Financial Times: September 19.

Lothian, N. (1984), How Companies Manage R&D. London: Institute of Cost and Management Accountants.

Maidique, M.A. (1980), Entrepreneurs champions and technological innovation. Sloan Management Review, (Winter): 59-76.

Midgley, D.F. (1977), Innovation and New Product Marketing. London: Croom Helm.

Miles, R.E. and C.C. Snow (1978), Organizational Structure, Strategy and Process. New York: McGraw Hill.

Miller, E. and P.H. Friesen (1982), Innovation in conservative and entrepreneurial firms: two models of strategic momentum. Strategic Management Journal, 3: 1-25.

Millman, A.F. (1982), Understanding barriers to product innovation at the R&D/Marketing interface. European Journal of Marketing, 16,5: 22-34.

Mintzberg, H., D. Raisinghani and A. Theoret (1976), The structure of "unstructured" decision processes. Administrative Science Quarterly, 21 (June): 246-275.

Muncaster, J.W. (1981), Picking new product opportunities. Research Management, XXIV,4 (Jan.): 26-29.

Nystrom, H. (1979), Creativity and Innovation. London: John Wiley.

Oakley, M. (1984), Managing Product Design. London: Weidenfeld & Nicholson.

Oakley, M.H. and W.H. Jones (1980), New product development and the venture concept. Management Research News, 3,1 (May): 12-13.

Parker, R.C. (1980), Guidelines for Product Innovation. London: British Institute of Management.

Parker, R.C. (1982), The Management of Innovation. Chichester: John Wiley & Sons.

Parkinson, S.T. (1982), The role of the user in successful new product development. R&D Management, 12,3: 123-131.

Bibliography and References

Parkinson, S.T. (1984), New Product Development in Engineering: comparison of the British and West German machine tool industries. Cambridge: Cambridge University Press.

Pascale, R.T. and A.G. Athos (1982), The Art of Japanese Management. Harmondsworth, Middlesex: Penguin.

Peters, T.J. & R.H. Waterman (1982), In Search of Excellence: Lessons from America's Best-run Companies. New York: Harper & Row.

Porter, M.E. (1980), Competitive Strategy. New York: The Free Press.

Pugh, D. et al. (1963), A schema for organization analysis. Administrative Science Quarterly, 8: 289-315.

Rafael, I.D. and A.H. Rubenstein (1984), Top management roles in R&D projects. R&D Management, 14,1: 37-46.

Ramo, S (1980), The Management of Innovative Technological Corporations. New York: John Wiley & Sons.

Randall, G (1980), Managing New Products. London: British Institute of Management Survey Report 47.

Roberts, E.B. (1979), Stimulating technological innovation - organizational approaches. Research Management, XXII,6 (Nov.): 26-30.

Rockwell, J.R. and M.C. Particelli (1982), New product strategy: how the pros do it. Industrial Marketing, (May): 49-60.

Rothberg, R. (ed.) (1976), Corporate Strategy and Product Innovation. New York: The Free Press.

Rothwell, R (1979), Successful and unsuccessful innovators. Planned Innovation, (April): 126-128.

Sands, S. (1983), Problems of organising for effective new product development. European Journal of Marketing, 17,4: 18-33.

Saren, M.A. (1984), A classification and review of models of the intra-firm innovation process. R&D Management, 14,1: 11-24.

Schmidt-Tiedermann, K.J. (1982), A new model of the innovation process. Research Management, XXV,2 (March): 18-21.

Schumacher, E.F. (1973), Small is Beautiful. New York: Harper & Row.

Schumpeter, J.A. (1962), Capitalism, Socialism and Democracy. New York: Harper & Row.

Shepard, H.A. (1967), Innovation resisting and innovation producing organizations. Journal of Business, (Oct.) 40: 470-477.

Souder, W.E. (1978), Effectiveness of product development methods. Industrial Marketing Management, 7: 299-307.

Souder, W.E. (1981), Encouraging entrepreneurship in large corporations. R&D Management, (May): 18-22.

Steele, L.W. (1975), Innovation in Big Business. New York: Elsevier.

Steiner, G.A. (1979), Strategic Planning. New York: The Free Press.

Stopford, J.M., J.H. Dunning and K.O. Haberich (1980), The World Directory of Multinational Enterprise. London: Macmillan.

Taylor, W.J. and T.F. Watling (1979), 2nd edition Successful Project Management. London: Business Books.

Townsend, J. et al. (1981), Innovations in Britain since 1945. Sussex University: Science Policy Research Unit. Occasional Paper No 16.

Twiss, B. (1980), 2nd edition, Managing Technological Innovation. London: Longman.

Bibliography and References

Urban, G.L. and J.R. Hauser (1980), Design and Marketing of New Products. Englewood Cliffs, N.J.: Prentice Hall.

Utterback, J.M. (1979), The dynamics of product and process innovation in industry, in Hill, C.T. & J.M. Utterback (eds.) (1979) Technological Innovation for a Dynamic Economy. New York: Pergamon: 40-65.

Utterback, J.M. and W.J. Abernathy (1975), A dynamic model of process and product innovation. Omega, 3,6: 639-656.

Verhage, B., Ph. Waalewijn and A.J. van Weele (1981), New product development in Dutch companies: the idea generation stage. European Journal of Marketing, 15.5: 73-85.

Watton, H.B. (1969), New Product Planning: A Practical Guide for Diversification. New Jersey: Prentice Hall.

Weber, M. (1921/1947), The Theory of Social and Economic Organization, translated by A.M. Henderson and T. Parsons. New York: The Free Press.

Wind, Y. (1982), Product Policy: Concepts, Methods and Strategy. Reading, Mass.: Addison-Wesley Publishing Co.

Zaltman, G., R. Duncan and J. Holbek (1973), Innovations and Organizations. New York: John Wiley & Sons.

INDEX

ATE   100, 101

bar chart   91
brainstorming   66, 87, 105, 133
business policy   8
business unit,   see SBU
British Telecom   128, 129, 132
bureaucratic communication   118

cash-cow products   114, 116, 128
centralisation   12-15, 36, 41, 43, 78
chief engineer   102, 103, 118
company self-renewal   7, 19, 160, 166
company stage of development   6, 83
competitive pressure   7,8
control manual, see development checklist

decentralisation   80
delegation of authority   12
design   98, 145, 146
development checklist   90, 105, 113
development time   71, 157, 158
DOI grants   106
dual control   15, 16, 22, 31

engineering manager,   see R&D manager

factoring   151
first names   63, 100
formal structures   49
formalisation   36, 40, 42

general manager   66, 68